Sᴛ. Lᴏᴜɪs Dᴀᴅ

St. Louis Dad

A Manual for New and Expecting Dads

by Kevin M. Mitchell

with Illustrations by Kevin Belford

Reedy Press

St. Louis, Missouri

Reedy Press
PO Box 5131
St. Louis, MO 63139

Library of Congress Control Number:
2007931128

ISBN: 978-1-933370-14-9

For information on all Reedy Press
publications visit our website at
www.reedypress.com.

Printed in the United States of America
07 08 09 10 11 5 4 3 2 1

CONTENTS

Preface
vii

Chapter One
What To Expect When Your
Wife Is Expecting
(Answer: One Grouchy Gal)
3

Chapter Two
The Moment of Truth, the First Three Months, and
Exactly Why It's Mustard Seed–Like
21

Chapter Three
Months 3–6, and Hey! There's a PERSON Emerging in
That Pooping, Eating, Sleeping Machine!
41

Chapter Four
Months 6–12, and Why Crawling Is Cute Until They
Actually Do It
57

Chapter Five
Months 12–18, and the Joy, Nay the Necessity, of Takeout
73

Chapter Six
Months 18–24: Too Early to Teach Them to Make a Martini?
89

Chapter Seven
*Terrible Twos, and Why a Do-It-Yourself Home
Vasectomy Is Looking Pretty Good*
105

Chapter Eight
*They Are Three! and Why the Wiggles Are a Threat to
Our National Sanity*
121

Chapter Nine
Four—The Age of "Because I Said So"
139

Chapter Ten
Five and Beyond
155

Appendix A
Are You SAHD Material?
169

Appendix B
*Especially Dad-Friendly Things to Do with Kids
under 5*
172

Acknowledgments
187

About the Author
188

PREFACE

As the story goes, my Mom had to leave me, in baby mode, with my dad to go to the store. She was gone a short time, and alas, I did what pediatricians call "poopy in the diaper." Dad did what any 35-year-old guy in 1965 would do: took me across the street to Mrs. Mays and made *her* change my diaper. And I wasn't even his first kid—I was his fourth! He made it through his entire adult life without changing a single diaper, and no one batted an eye.

Boy, have things changed. First and foremost, Mrs. Mays no longer changes my diapers. Second, while St. Louis dads may still depend on the kindness of neighbor ladies in this especially friendly town, they are expected to take a more active part in raising their children.

I have mixed feelings about this. Those of us who grew up in the late twentieth century remember different dads from what we're expected to be. There were the Cardinal games, the little league soccer tournaments, and the afternoons spent fetching Stag beer from a profoundly decaled cooler for Dad and various "uncles" named Kenny, Harry, and Lefty. Otherwise, basically Dad went to work, came home, had a beer, ate dinner, and maybe you'd watch M*A*S*H together, but that was about it.

But we have "evolved" and are expected to be more involved in the life of the child. Also, as the husband-wife relationship went from noble-serf to partner-partner or even yin-yang, more is expected of us.

Here is where I'm supposed to say that this is an "opportunity" or some such politically correct thing. But this is a guy book, and I'm aiming to tell it as it is: Babies are disruptive, disgusting little creatures. But hey! They are *your* disruptive, disgusting little creatures! And there is a reality that the more bonding, more participating you can do with the newborn, the better adjusted the kid will be. That's a fact—just recently the World Health Organization confirmed that a child's growth is influenced more by environmental factors than genetics in the first five years, and a child's personality is almost completely developed by then. So consider being part of it all as much as possible.

And I'm evidence that this can be done, that you can be a supportive spouse and loving dad from day one without completely losing your frickin' mind.*

So I'm using this "manual," if you will, to basically share everything I wish I knew before I descended into this chaos. It takes into consideration the cultural and social atmosphere unique to the Gateway to the West, and what I hope is even more helpful, specific ideas for what to do with the kids. At the time of publication, there is not yet a bar that also has a playroom for toddlers and a big TV blaring ESPN. But if everyone reading this buys 10 copies, and gets 10 of their friends to buy 10 copies times infinity, I promise to open one.

Man, won't that be cool.

*my therapist insisted on the word "completely" for legal purposes.

ST. LOUIS DAD

In every family crisis situation, I've always asked myself what TV's Jim Anderson would have done on Father Knows Best. *Of course! Just smile at my wife, Margaret, pat Kitten on the head, and put everything back together again. Then have a very calm, man-to-man talk with errant son, Bud. Unfortunately, my Bud and Kitten have formed all their ideas about Dad from TV's* Married with Children.

—Don Corrigan, publisher, *Webster-Kirkwood Times*

Chapter One

What to Expect When Your Wife Is Expecting

(Answer: One Grouchy Gal)

It's real. You're going to be a Dad. Maybe this is planned and there's been lots of peeing on the proverbial stick from Walgreens. Is it yellow? Is it green? Wait a minute—it appears to be turquoise. Does that mean you're just kinda pregnant?

The first reality to accept is you are now unceremoniously demoted. Your Kingdom Company is now Baby, Inc., and when the dust from merger settles, you'll realize you are now in fact a minority shareholder. You can advise, consult, and she'll likely ask your input, but somewhat disconcerting is that she gets all the final decision-making power, from what color to paint the baby room (she'll want seafoam green; you'll want Cardinal red), to whether you are getting fudge ripple ice cream or cheesecake. It's just nature's way.

Didja Know?

While pregnant ladies make weak point guards in pickup basketball, they make terrific designated drivers!

Bud Light: Now This One, and That One, Are for You!

One of the first noticeable changes is that she is no longer bogarting your Bud Light. The data is in, and it's strongly recommended that pregnant women abstain from drinking completely. The obvious immediate benefit is that there's more for you. The downside is, now Miss Carrie Nation is suddenly going to take notice in your exuberant

As your gal pal will be gaining up to 25 to 35 pounds, a comment like, "Man, your ass is the size of a Ford Explorer!" is tempting to make. This seemingly innocent comment, surprisingly, often is the cause of instant crying and/or a frying pan to the head. So it's not recommended.

drinking, and you're suddenly not quite as funny as you were just a month or so ago.

A true gentleman, in the spirit of solidarity, would show support for the woman and abstain from drinking, too. Luckily, though, this book isn't for gentlemen, so you're off the hook.

Still, include her as much as possible in the fun via virgin drinks and non-alcoholic beer (but stay away from that non-alcoholic wine—it's totally disgusting).

Also, be prepared for—and supportive of—the food choices changing in your fridge. Modern medical professionals have mind-boggling abilities to scare the hell out of everyone about everything. It's like nobody had a baby before you so they don't want to take any chances. One of the many surprise decrees is that suddenly deli meat is a killer. Also on the list is feta cheese. Of course, you being logical, you're thinking if pregnant women can't eat those things, there'd be no Jareds of Subway. But alas, the medical profession has left all logic behind in getting that baby out of your partner, so be prepared to go through this entire period with a question mark on your face.

"Sympathy Weight"

Missing those days when you and your buds would be sitting around in a sea of Busch cans and suddenly getting the munchies and running to White Castle at two in the morning? The good news is that those days are back. Woo hoo! The bad news is that instead of a sea of Busch cans you're actually in bed, fast asleep. And you have to go to work in a few hours.

Food that usually wasn't present in the house will suddenly be appearing—you'll find out, yes, you can buy Ted Drewes in your grocery's freezer section. Nature's little reward for her throwing up, getting largely uncomfortable, and having this growing creature push on her bladder until it's the size of a pea, is she gets all these fun cravings, and society encourages—nay, celebrates!—them.

What's in this for you? Well, you become more than just a delivery boy. You also end up "supporting" her and partaking in the munch-fest as well. Yes, that is her eating Imo's Double Meat Deluxe at 11:00 a.m. on a Saturday after a large breakfast and right before lunch. But if you start "helping her out" by eating the second half all the time, well, you're on the road to what we call "sympathy weight."

Fun Virgin Drink Recipes for Her

Safe Sex on the Beach
2 oz of cranberry juice
2 oz grapefruit or orange juice
1 oz peach nectar

Virgin Pina Colada
7 oz pineapple juice
2 oz coconut cream
1 cup crushed ice
Blend at high speed

Yellowjacket
2 oz pineapple juice
2 oz orange juice
1-½ oz lemon juice
Pour into cocktail shaker half filled with ice cubes, shake well. Strain into a glass of ice.

Virgin Margarita
1 oz lime juice
1 oz orange juice
3 oz (non-alcoholic) sour mix
Pour into cocktail shaker half filled with ice cubes, shake well. Strain into a margarita glass with ice. Don't forget to salt the glass!

Texas Sunrise
8 oz orange juice
¾ oz grenadine syrup
Crushed ice

Beer
Note: Non-alcoholic beer actually has around .5% alcohol (regular beer has closer to 5%). The better ones include Kaliber, Buckler, St. Paulie's N/A, O'Doul's Amber.

Wine
All non-alcoholic wine is gross.

Not sure why they call it that, but it's typical for guys to gain weight during pregnancy too. And in a town where they fry pretty much anything and tell you it's "toasted," it's a particularly dangerous situation. Whatever exercise routine you're in now is going to get disrupted soon enough when the baby comes. So now is the time to hit the "Y" and keep up with your softball or basketball schedule.

Is It a He or a She? And What to Call the Thing?

Few decisions cause more angst than whether or not to find out the baby's sex. Some people need to know. Some want to be surprised.

One father-to-be insisted he find out the sex so that the boy or girl as a newborn, screaming, bloody mess didn't sense "one second of disappointment or pick up any negative vibe upon being born." (Yes, as

Didja Know?

As of this writing, it'll cost around $606,000 to raise a kid in St. Louis to age 18, batteries not included. Luckily, you don't have to pay this all at once, and there's a $1 off coupon in the back of this book that should help.

(Source: babycenter.com/costofchild)

a matter of fact he *was* from California). The phrase "we don't care as long as he or she is healthy" is common and sincere, though if it helps, little girls don't pee in your face when you're changing their diaper and little boys end up costing less over the 18 years you're responsible for them.

This is a case where, whoever feels stronger about whether or not to find out usually gets their way. Of course, typically, the woman tends to feel stronger about it than the guy, but really, it's fun either way.

Then there's the name. Again, another personal decision that often becomes a bit of a battle between the parents-to-be. Yes, we all loved your Great Uncle Adolph Stalin Kopecki, but maybe there are other ways to honor him than using his name. And she might bring equally challenging names to the table, like "Forrest" . . . eventually of course you'll compromise, she'll come to her senses, and you can eagerly welcome Albert Pujols Kopecki into the world.

Some people think it's romantic to wait until the baby is born to see what it looks like and then name him or her. This can be dangerous and has led to quite a few "Slimyplacentacovereduterusdropping Kopecki," which, of course, is hard to spell.

Whatever it is, if and when you and your gal decide on a name, DON'T TELL ANYONE. Wait until the baby is born. No matter how perfect the name is, someone will give you a reason to dislike it. "Oh, I knew a Zachary once," they'll say upon hearing it. "He would never buy a round of beer when it was his turn, and later went on to cannibalize a family of Quakers."

Popular Names

Missouri

Boys		Girls	
Jacob	Ryan	Emma	Taylor
Ethan	Nicolas	Madison	Chloe
Andrew	Austin	Emily	Anna
Tyler	Samuel	Abigail	Sarah
Michael	Alexander	Olivia	Sophia
William	James	Hannah	Lauren
Joseph	Zachary	Grace	Isabella
Joshua	Dylan	Alexis	Samantha
Logan	John	Elizabeth	Hailey
Matthew	Caleb	Alyssa	Ella

Illinois

Boys		Girls	
Michael	Nicolas	Emily	Hannah
Jacob	Ethan	Emma	Sarah
Daniel	David	Olivia	Alexis
Anthony	William	Abigail	Alyssa
Joshua	Tyler	Madison	Jessica
Alexander	Christopher	Grace	Anna
Matthew	John	Isabella	Sophia
Joseph	James	Ashley	Lauren
Andrew	Nathan	Elizabeth	Natalie
Ryan	Jonathan	Samantha	Kayla

Source: Social Security Online, www.ssa.gov

BUT nobody ever says anything bad about a baby name when it's attached to an actual cute baby. So even if the name is "Mussolini," it's "Mussolini! That's so cute! Look at him!"

Labor Help

You may be relieved or you may be miffed (or likely both) if your wife has considered bringing in a pinch-hitter.

Sometimes it's the Mom that is not your Mom. Touchy situation, but hopefully you can avoid that for reasons that should be painfully obvious. Sometimes you'll hear words like "midwife" and "doula." Consider these people subcontractors who are actually better at showing up when they are supposed to than the clown scheduled to resurface your driveway.

A midwife is a woman who assists in the birth and is responsible for the health and safety of mother and baby. They are big on prenatal care and work to reduce C-section rates, traumatic deliveries, and questionable or unnecessary medical intervention. Until very

---

DIDJA KNOW?

While it might seem logical that the term "baby-proofing" would mean to make one's place of dwelling safe from a baby's ability to infiltrate it, it actually means something entirely different! Oh, if it were only that; but alas, it means that your house must be safe from the not-so-proverbial lost eye, gouged cheek, or major concussion. Funny, but true!

recently, being a midwife without a Certified Nurse Midwife license was considered a felony in Missouri, but recent legislation with bipartisan support changed that. But those who oppose midwives have turned to courts to keep it illegal (and keep home births more difficult). For current information on this go to www .friendsofmomidwives.org.

A doula is a midwife, but in a more granola-chomping and Birkenstock-wearing way, and with typically less clinical and nursing training. She supplies physical and emotional support and says "it's going to be okay" a lot. Often a doula is teamed up with a certified midwife.

There are several good reasons to get involved with either of the above:

- Your partner wants to have a home birth.
- You and your partner want to have the least intrusive birth possible.
- You travel a lot and can't guarantee you'll be there for the birth.

Fun Fact!

What's the difference between a baby gate and a dog gate? Answer: About $30! Yes, that's right—the gates you can buy at PetSmart usually work just as well as those you buy at Babies "R" Us. And by doing this, not only do you save some money, but you also bolster your case for naming the newborn "Fido."

There's also one really bad reason to get involved with either of the above:

- You're completely and utterly lame-o.

If you're the type of guy who absolutely refuses to call in someone and pay him to rewire an outlet, build a patio deck, or hang a new storm door, but you're "not comfortable" getting involved with this home improvement project, then you need a severe attitude adjustment, soldier. Now, a chick would say that the birth of another living creature is the most amazing beautiful blah blah experience you could ever blah blah in your life. Well, it's actually stressful, tedious, scary, and totally disgusting—but until the DNA samples from the lab prove otherwise, you were there at the conception of this thing, so you should be there when it comes out. Partner with the midwife or doula, don't have her replace you.

GETTING SOME CLASS

And this might not be something you want to wing. It requires planning. More planning than a poker night, but less than a typical Rams tailgate party. So trust us when we assure you that you're completely capable of it.

Still, for better or for worse (and for reasons that will become apparent later, the jury is still out on this), you'll be in the room when the whole thing goes down, as opposed to the Tin Can Tavern knockin' back PBRs waiting for the call.

There are many great institutions in St. Louis that offer childbirth classes. No matter what your role is going to be, you should attend one with your wife. Here are just a few that offer classes:

- St. Anthony's Hospital (www.stanthonysmedcenter.com)
- Missouri Baptist Center (www.missouribaptistmedicalcenter.org)
- DePaul Health Center (www.ssmdepaul.com/internet/home/depaul.nsf)
- St. Elizabeth's in Belleville (www.steliz.org)
- Barnes Jewish (BJC) (several locations) (www.bjc.org)

If you're going to have a hospital delivery, it's best to take a class there, when available. Also, A Labor of Love in Wentzville (www.a-laboroflove.com) offers a variety of classes.

Get your hands dirty with this and take a class. Will it do any good? Maybe. It's sorta like driver's ed in high school: It doesn't really teach to you drive, but it gets you in the right frame of mind, plus you get to see totally gross movies.

THE BABY SHOWER

In one of the sorriest developments in western civilization ever, men are now often invited to and expected to attend baby showers. Run SCREAMING. Otherwise you'll be sentenced to standing around going, "Oh yes, that's cute. Yes, that's cute. Oh, that's so cute," as she takes PAINFULLY LONG to open presents. And you know why everything is so damn cute? It's only because it's TINY. See, babies, relative to adults or your average Humvee, are TINY. So things for them are also TINY. For women, Tiny = Cute. As in: "Look at these little sockies! They're so cute!" "Look at this little Cardinals cap! It's so cute!" "Aww . . . wittle baby nunchucks. Look, honey, aren't these cute?"

You sit there comatose, this Mona Lisa smile set on your face, gently bobbing your head for what will seem like an eternity. Then, you'll have to haul all the crap out to the car.

Unless one of the baby shower games involves playing Quarters, it's worth coming up with any excuse to get out of it . . . even if it's, "Gee, I'd love to, but I'm finally going to baby-proof the house!"

BABY-PROOFING THE HOUSE

Because you're born with male genitals and a penchant for power tools, you will suddenly be faced with the herculean task of baby-proofing your home. Suddenly, thanks to the savvy marketers of Baby Products You Don't Need But Feel You Must Urgently Pay A Premium Price For Or You're A Horrible Horrible Excuse For A Man, *everything* in your house is suddenly going to *kill your newborn baby*. That electrical outlet? Of course Albert will find a stray fork and stick it in. That toilet? Oh, god, surely little Claire will spontaneously jump in, flush herself down, and be wrestling with alligators in the Mississippi before you notice she's gone.

Oh, and that coffee table? Pre-conception, it was a handy piece of furniture on which to stack your issues of *Sporting News*; now it's a maniacal, dangerous, sharp-corner-wielding machine that will not only endanger the very life of your precious Albert, it will keep him out of an Ivy League college.

However, just because scaring you into buying their products is the inspiration for Babies "R" Us profit margins, a little common sense at this point is not a bad idea. For one thing, think about what your house looked like when you were a baby. You made it out relatively okay and what, there were not only exposed outlets, but your Mom had that beloved rug made out of rusty nails and shards of glass. Something like that.

So this is what you do: Crawl around on the floor and see things from a baby point of view. Anything that is dangerous or precious, move above that level. This includes your CD collection, especially if you alphabetize.

The absolute most important things to be concerned about include:

- Chemicals and drugs. Definitely install locks on the doors to the cabinet under the sink that contains cleaning products. Also, if you keep anything under the sink in the bathroom, that needs to be locked.
- Bookshelves. They need to be fastened to the wall. Sooner than you realize (and sooner than you'd like) that baby will be up on two feet and pulling at things, and that includes shelves that could topple over on him.
- Stairways. Install a gate. Sure, we all enjoy a tumble down the stairs, but for your newborn, let's postpone it for as long as possible.

There's a ton more money you can spend, but we say use your guy-given common sense.

Car Seat Installation

When I was born, my Mom tossed me in a laundry basket and took me home in the car. That explains a lot, including my irrational fear of fabric softeners.

Now, the St. Louis–area hospitals won't let you take the baby home unless you show up with a properly installed car seat. And it is serious business, as our Children's Hospital points out that 80 percent of the car seats they inspect aren't put in correctly. The stakes are high, and you've likely never known the fear of God until you realize it's two weeks from the baby's birth and you don't have the damn thing in.

First off, get a good new one, not a used one. Read the online reviews and talk to your baby-making friends. Then, prepare to sweat bullets trying to figure it out before finally seeking help with it. Now, the doctors and nurses will tell you that any local fire house will help you install it correctly, but that's not entirely true. Try calling a few in your neighborhood and you might get lucky, otherwise keep your eyes and ears open for hospitals that will help. Children's is one that frequently has free sessions (www.stlouischildrens.org), though an appointment is needed. St. Joseph in Kirkwood (www.stjoseph kirkwood.com) is another that offers help from a certified car seat installer.

But don't procrastinate. Typically, these sessions are offered only once a month or less often, and only for a few hours.

TALK TO THE BELLY

Finally, it's not too soon to start talking to the baby or even reading to it. Yes, they can really hear you in there (so watch it, potty mouth, because the rug-rat-to-be can distinguish between her voice and yours). Let's have them used to your voice nice and early. Ask them how they are doing, ask if they are ready to come out, read them the Cardinal stats, and even sing to the belly. Appropriate songs: Nursery rhymes, Woody Guthrie songs, jazz standards. Sammy Hagar tunes? . . . maybe not so much.

If you're of a typical St. Louis-guy size, this might backfire in that your partner will want to talk to *your* belly. This is to be discouraged at all costs. It's not the least bit amusing. Besides, that Chicken Fiesta Burrito might just start talking back, and that would be embarrassing to everyone involved, especially the burrito.

THE WAIT

As you get closer, your gal is likely going to get more and more anxious. Her "nesting" impulses will kick in and this is one to-do you should stay on top of getting ready for the new arrival. Also, try to comfort her and keep her as calm as possible. It helps if you don't freak out.

Stick around, too—not a time to plan that weekend away, even if it is deer hunting season.

And . . . just . . . wait.

Chapter One
Review Questions

1. Your newly pregnant partner suddenly makes a great:
   - A. Monster truck rally stunt driver
   - B. Rodeo clown
   - C. Designated driver
   - D. Raspberry soufflé

2. Which is the least dangerous to refer to as a "pig"?
   - A. Your local police officer
   - B. A K-SHE 95 DJ
   - C. The woman carrying the seed of your loins
   - D. The woman carrying your third order of hot wings

3. What is not a popular St. Louis–area name for a baby?
   - A. Logan
   - B. Taylor
   - C. Alyssa
   - D. Sputnik

4. A doula is to a pregnant lady, what:
   - A. a White Castle "belly bomber" is to indigestion
   - B. a hamster is to a gerbil
   - C. a spatula is to a pair of over-easy eggs
   - D. a Charles Dooley is to a Francis Slay

5. Short Essay: Compare and contrast your pregnant gal's wild hormonal mood swings to the 2006 Blues hockey season.

The working hours in a television newsroom are long . . . even weird by some 9-to-5 standards. So I didn't have as much time with my kids as they were growing up as I would have liked to have had. But our little family worked very hard during the girls' pre-teen years to slip away on Saturdays to some of our favorite haunts so I could get updates on what was going on in their lives. And they could find out some of the things going on in mine of which I thought they might find some interest.

On those sacred Saturdays you could find us (and we hoped you couldn't) having a burger, fries, and shake at the Ground Round on Clayton Road, a double scoop of ice cream at the Dairy Queen on Big Bend at Wydown, bagels and cream cheese at Posh Nosh in Clayton (the girls didn't prefer pastrami and corn beef like their Dad), and our most favorite hideaway, Oak Knoll Park in Clayton where we would often have a picnic lunch and the young Hunter girls would craft "boats" out of twigs and leaves and race them in the park's pond.

—Julius Hunter, veteran St. Louis news journalist

Chapter Two

The Moment of Truth, the First Three Months, and Exactly Why It's Mustard Seed-like

We're not going to spend a lot of time on the actual birth. It's like a bad accident, meeting the person of your dreams, or a "wave" at the new Busch Stadium—no time to really think about it, you just gotta react.

The first part is critical: You have to show up. No golf weekends, no trips to Chicago to see the Blues and the Blackhawks play, and no business trips to Vegas can be planned. You're a man. You started this, so you gotta to see it through.

Despite the training, the classes, and the talks you've had with others, when you're in the hospital room, the birthing room, your bedroom with a midwife, or the back seat of your Dodge Neon on Highway 44, you'll quickly realize how tiny your role really is. You'll pine for the days when fathers-to-be sat in a smoky tavern kicking back shots, wearing those cool hats they wore in the 1940s, and waiting for The Phone Call. Or at least in the waiting room with a copy of the *Sporting News* and a pocket full of Swisher Sweets.

But alas, you're required to be in the trenches. Despite dutifully muttering, "breathe, honey," as you were trained to do from class, you're pretty much at batboy status.

Specifically, you are to:

- Stay the hell out of the way of the nurses and doctors
- Have a bottle of water handy
- Wonder where your one-time blushing bride learned that kind of language and if she kisses her mudder with dat mouth

And most important:

- Witness the kind of pain you've put her through. She will make references to it to you and the kid for the rest of her life

Things to Bring to the Hospital

- Magazines
- Books
- Music
- Healthy snacks (granola bars, rice cakes, etc.)
- Phone numbers (people to call to announce the big news)
- Videos (most hospital rooms have video players, believe it or not—but bring something for her, a romantic comedy like *When Harry Met Sally*, as opposed to *Dirty Harry*)

During labor, just be as supportive and upbeat as possible—but not *too* upbeat, as that will piss her off. Be helpful, but not *too* helpful—that will piss her off. Just exist, but don't exist *too* much—that will definitely piss her off.

Finally, don't freak out at the globby mess that eventually comes out of her. It's not pretty, clean, and cute like in the movies. It's a mess—but it's your mess. So congratulations!

Also, you'll be like, "Damn, junior is well hung, just like his dad!" Not so fast, Einstein. That's just the umbilical cord.

Fun Fact!

Debate rages as to whether a newborn looks most like Mom or Dad, but in fact, social scientists have concluded that 92.7 percent of all newborns look like Howie Mandel.

A C-Section

We're not talking about where those who have game tickets between sections B and D sit—we're talking about something much more serious. A C-section, or Cesarean section, is about as intrusive as you can get. The woman is cut open at the belly and the baby is yanked out rather than going through the birth canal (vaginal birth).

Usually they come about when there is a problem—labor is slow, the baby has an abnormal heart rate, the baby is the size of a pony keg and just too big to come out the "regular" way. There are many who feel C-sections are done too frequently. The World Health Organization states that no region in the world is justified in having a Cesarean rate greater than 10 to 15 percent, yet in the last 20 years Cesarean rates in the U.S. have quintupled to 23.8 percent (source: childbirth.org). There are health risks, especially to the not-so-little lady, so any talk of planning one just for convenience's sake . . . well, try to let nature take its course. It's less traumatic for all involved, especially the baby.

But there are situations where it's absolutely necessary, and when that happens, be prepared to be especially supportive—and sleep even less. The stay in the hospital will be a few days longer, and full recovery will be four to six weeks at least. You need to be on hand to do *all* the shopping, cooking, and (gulp) cleaning (good news—she'll be in no position to bend down and see that you didn't vacuum under the coffee table . . . or under *anything* for that matter).

BREAST-FEEDING

Political correctness be damned: Breast-feeding should be avoided. It's hard, inconvenient, and hurts like hell. Don't you do it. Let *her* do it, and you keep your nipples—whatever the hell they are actually for—to yourself.

One of the many shocking things you'll learn in these early days is that a lot of women actually have trouble breast-feeding. You'd think there shouldn't be anything more natural, but there it is—she's trying and other women are coming in and grabbing your spouse's breast and manipulating it like a bocce ball.

This is another in a series of unsettling situations where there's not a damn thing you can do but be "supportive" and "encouraging." It doesn't matter how many accessories your tool belt has, if the breast-feeding thing doesn't come easy, it can be upsetting and frustrating to the woman. But the rewards—both with the baby's health and, to be blunt, the checkbook—are huge.

THE FIRST FEW DAYS

Now that you're a dad, the first thing you have to do is deal with the in-laws. See, they just got promoted. Prior to birth, they were the somewhat annoying beings who happened to give birth to your spouse. Now they are GRANDPARENTS, complete with themed sweatshirts and car bumper stickers declaring them as such. Apparently, they also get a

DIDJA KNOW?

In some ancient cultures, after the birth, the father would gather up the placenta and cook it with wild yams and cilantro. Clearly, though, this was before toasted ravioli was invented; so instead, celebrate the birth with an order at your favorite sports bar.

"Get Into Your House Free" card, so expect to see them more often than before. . . . Just remember, in twenty or thirty years you'll get to do the same to see *your* grandchild, so be polite, smile a lot, and make sure you have new games to play on your Playstation.

There'll be others wanting to visit, and you need to be the policeman. Allow only a few visits, and keep them short unless you *want* them to see a gaggle of nurses parade in, inspect your wife's hoo-ha, inquire about her bowel movements, and admonish you for sneaking a beer into the hospital. Encourage people instead to come visit once you get home.

Meanwhile, various hospital personnel will keep taking the baby places for various things. Speak up often, and ask a lot of questions. Some of it may be more intrusive than you want, or your gal will be asking you what the nurse said about the perineal tears three hours later. In fact, take notes!

SLEEP—OR LACK THEREOF

It's a pretty amazing time, those first few weeks. No doubt for months before the birth, people will taunt you with, "Get some sleep now because none will happen after the baby's born." No doubt you're thinking, mostly correctly, "I've stayed up all night cramming for tests, on road trips to Colorado, and for *Three Stooges* marathons. I can handle this."

But then by the third or fourth week of getting up every few hours, it'll hit you: Oh wow, man, this is *forever.*

There are two extreme situations that you will find yourself in—and ideally these have been discussed with your wife at some point:

- You're the one with the job, while she's "on vacation" and thus 100 percent in charge of Albert.
- You're getting up every single time, either instead of her or with her, whenever Claire needs something, which is like, every nine minutes.

There are advantages and disadvantages to both. The first scenario makes you wide-eyed and bushy tailed, singing, "Baby? What baby?" The downside is that there is important bonding going on during these times, and it would be a shame for you to miss out on it.

The more practical side is, if you do take the old-school approach, then you're left with this thing in your house that you just see from a distance, always bobbing its head, drooling, not able to focus . . . and that thing is taking care of your baby!

Typically, the mother of your child is on some sort of maternity leave and doesn't have to work with heavy machinery, land a jet at the airport, or attend a St. Louis School Board meeting—life-threatening stuff. So if you don't fall into one of those categories, and you can take a turn at least once in a while, everyone benefits.

Even if she's breast-feeding, it's not like there's nothing for you to do. Getting up with her in the middle of the night can actually be more than just moral support . . . oddly, the little creature will often fall asleep sometime between breast number one and breast number two and will need to be awakened. As a St. Louis guy, you're likely good at being loud. But not too loud . . . a little "na na na na, na na na na, hey, hey, stay awake" or perhaps a few bars from your favorite Green Day tune should do the trick . . . or, the kid might need changing.

I know what you're thinking: "But I love little Albert just the way he is!"

We're not talking that kind of changing.

DIAPERS, DIAPERS, EVERYWHERE

Real men change diapers; it's a number one priority in situations involving number two.

There are three choices:

- You buy cloth diapers and handle the laundering of them yourself. Advantages: It's the least expensive route, it's the most environmentally friendly option, and the biggest bonus, said baby becomes potty-trained quicker (the local diaper service says up to a year earlier).

Disadvantage: Must have a lot of time and an extremely strong constitution (see "Didja Know," page 31).

- You go with a diaper service. To show what a demand for this there is, there is now only one—count 'em, one!—diaper service in St. Louis. It's **Baby Care** at 314.732.7009. Advantage: Same as number one, but of course, they supply fresh, clean diapers and pick up the dirty ones on a weekly basis. Disadvantage: Better not forget to put the huge bag of stinky, soiled diapers out that day!
- Buy disposable diapers. Advantage: This is the easiest of the three. Disadvantage: You'll quickly fill up a landfill with these things, and most agree it's the most expensive route—how *much* more expensive, however, is debatable. Diaper services make the case that they're cheaper, especially when you factor in pail and liner savings and the fact that babies are toilet trained sooner with cloth.

Cloth diapers are more comfortable on the baby, and those who can go this route swear that babies who wear them get potty trained faster. Why? Because the technology that goes into the modern diaper rivals what is happening in the genetics labs of Washington University. The said poop and pee can linger comfortably in the baby's pants for hours and hours. With cloth, the baby feels it immediately, and eventually that will make him realize that maybe he needs to figure out the toilet thing rather than sit around in his own waste.

Otherwise, the environmental difference between cloth and disposable seems slight—yes, disposables take up less landfill space, but aren't you using a ton of water and energy to run those washers and dryers?

Another thing: Buy the 128-pack—or bigger. This, like beer, really needs to be bought in bulk. Where to get them: Consider a Costco membership.

Also, Toys "R" Us / Babies "R" Us typically have competitive prices for these things. In a sneaky bit of store design, they purposely put them in the very back, making one walk through the entire store filled with all these "cute" things. . . . Some women can't resist picking up some accessories while there, and that's how they get you. Guys can walk through without batting an eye, so maybe you should be the one to buy the diapers. . . .

Finally, think hard before going generic. Diapers are bad enough, but leaky ones are particularly gruesome. Make the investment.

Slimed

While we're on the subject, lots of odd things come spewing out your baby's various orifices, and you will get slimed—slimed good, and slimed often. It's a good idea to invest in a dozen cloth diapers to have around for this adventure in regurgitation. We're not saying to not love your baby, just treat her like a loaded weapon. You'll come home from work with your favorite tie and a freshly pressed new shirt you just bought at Dillard's, and that innocent, beautiful Claire will just light up and smile with such a ray of love you'll have to pick her up.

Then, she'll Linda Blair all over you.

So always grab the cloth diaper or a burp cloth of some kind (this spit-up is highly toxic, so paper towels won't do). Put it on your shoulder when you pick the kid up. It'll save on your dry cleaning bills.

Didja Know?

You are entering an exciting era where you spend an excessive amount of time discussing poop, poop-related products, and the quality or lack of aforementioned poop. Here are the Top 10 most commonly used words and phrases you'll need to know when conversing on this thrilling, fun-filled topic:

- Tiny
- Big
- Huge Blowout
- Oh Dear God, You Change Her
- Lime Green
- Mustard-Seedy
- Totally Disgusting—I Mean It, You Change Her
- Runny
- Wet
- Texture Is Rubbery, Aroma Fruity with a Hint of Dark Chocolate, with a Certain *Je Ne Sais Quoi* That Reminds Me of the Monsanto Chemical Plants off Highway 55
- I Must Now Proceed to Blow My Lunch, You Change Her For the Love of God Please

SCREAMING & CRYING

Another thing that is hard to appreciate until you're there in the foxhole with it is the sheer volume these little things can achieve. The loudness can rival a Sammy Hagar concert and can be as appealing as a drunken Michael Anthony.

In fact, it can be downright unnerving. This is something you, as the St. Louis Guy, need to step up to. Most of the time, the woman portion of this program gets, understandably, completely unraveled at this. You, however, must remain calm. You must tell her what she's already read a zillion times: This is how the little beings communicate. They scream when they are hungry. And when they are uncomfortable. Or tired. Or bored.

Or, sometimes they just cry.

The least manly thing you can do is to join in with the scream-fest, especially something aimed at your spouse—you know, something like, "CAN YOU PLEASE MAKE THAT BABY STOP CRYING," generously sprinkled with off-color terms your high school football coach used when you lost against Parkway West. This contributes to what we shall call "a bad vibe" and makes things worse. Instead, you need to remain calm and steadfast as you work through a variety of options.

Picking up the baby and pacing usually works, though some prefer to let him or her "cry it out." Rocking works, feeding works, some like to go with a pacifier. But no matter what, STAY CALM and do not become unnerved. The screaming is just a part of the whole baby deal.

Car rides often put screaming babies to sleep. Even at two in the morning, guys will throw said baby in the car seat, fire up the car, and go for a spin. But it doesn't have to be a total loss— hit the drive-thru of your not-so-local White Castle and load up on Belly Bombers!

"You Gotta See the Baby"

Friends, family, neighbors, coworkers, Mongolian hordes, and mortgage brokers will likely crawl out of the woodwork and descend on your house in the first three months because they "gotta see the baby." The better-bred ones will bring food, which you'll be grateful for because there's not a lot of cooking going on during this time.

Please be especially cautious when a female-type visits, especially when there are more than one of them. Stay calm, but politely excuse yourself to your basement, your baseball game, or even your orthodontist, because women LOVE to go over and over the gory details of the birth. Yes, these same gals who can't watch a Mel Gibson movie all the way through without the palm of their hand planted over their face, will now suddenly revel in all the disgusting details of the birth. If you get stuck in the room, you'll have to relive the gruesome event *ad nauseam*.

Your job when women show up is to be pleasant, show off the baby, explain why you named her what you did, see that they have a beverage, and get lost for about two hours.

"Good Baby" vs. "Bad Baby"

You will be surprised when you get asked: "So is he a good baby?" We suggest the reply, "He's okay, but he's hard to start on cold mornings and gets lousy gas mileage."

The interloper is actually asking whether the baby is quiet, passive, sleeps all the time. If that's what you were after, you would have just gone to the Humane Society and picked up a fourteen-year-old cat named Sanborn rather than chosen to raise a child. Sure, some babies are incrementally more "convenient" than others, but don't ever let anyone pull the good/bad thing on you. There's no such thing as a bad baby, except maybe Rosemary's Baby, but we think even *he* was just misunderstood.

So when someone asks, "Is it a good baby or a bad baby?" simply say, "All babies are good babies."

Your Relationship with Mom

Be aware that these baby creatures, while seeming primitive, are actually unusually sensitive. From here on out, be especially conscious of moods, inflections, body language, and wall-punching. No yelling, name-calling, or frantic waving of the arms about the head and neck area in a negative manner.

Keeping your typically cool head is crucial here, and providing this new creature with a serene and confident demeanor will go a long way in the child's development.

So:

WRONG: [screaming] "GET IN HERE! This thing just crapped all over my *Sports Illustrated* swimsuit issue! I SAID GET IN HERE . . . NOW!"

RIGHT: [baby talk] "Oh lovee, might I have a moment of your time? I wish to show you this astonishing fecal work of art that our genius little one masterminded on my silly old periodical."

Babies start learning immediately from Mom and Dad about how to be, and how you and the little lady interact with each other imprints on them from day one. So straighten up and fly right.

DIDJA KNOW?

Babies love to be thrown in the air and caught! (Who doesn't love this? The Mom-type person. So simply do it when she's out of the room.) How high? It depends on the weight of the baby, the velocity, and the wind currents.

Do they enjoy being punted? Er, not so much. So remember to take the *football*, not the baby, to the Punt, Pass, & Kick contest held at your old high school.

Parents as Teachers

Parents as Teachers is a terrific organization that we're lucky to have available in St. Louis. It's a FREE service provided by state grants that allows parent educators to visit families with newborns. Communities such as Bayless, Brentwood, Clayton, Kirkwood, Maplewood/Richmond Heights, St. Louis City, and Webster Groves have their own websites. Wherever you live in the area, you can get hooked up with the organization through its national site at wwwparentsasteachers.org.

Once you are enrolled, they assign a professional case worker who comes to your home a couple of times a year and provides ideas to help with the baby's development. They answer questions and provide tip sheets about ways to play with the baby and deal with typical challenges (sleeping, eating, potty training, etc.). Also, they are trained to spot any possible developmental problems early, and in the rare instance that there is something that needs to be addressed, they can get your child the help he or she needs to minimize any issues later. Definitely take advantage of this; in addition to the visits, they offer helpful workshops and even fun concerts and events.

Where You Can Take a
0–3 Month Old

First of all, Mom is likely not going to feel like going anywhere for at least six weeks. Then a bit of cabin fever will hit, and/or she'll want a little alone time.

The misconception is that the cute little thing is a huge albatross the second it pops out of the womb, but actually, all she's doing is sleeping, pooping, and eating. So this is really your last chance to gain some semblance of your pre-procreation days. Throw the kid in the car seat and go to a restaurant, friend's house, or coffee place. It's pretty easy.

Obviously, the kid will be noise- and smoke-sensitive, so places like the Creepy Crawl or Harrah's are off limits. Also, almost every place in Sauget is likely inappropriate, as are some of the less-family-friendly tattoo parlors. If you dine in Ballwin or Arnold, great news! Smoking in restaurants is outlawed in those communities. Otherwise, a list of smoke-free restaurants and bars in St. Louis can be found at www.breatheasymo.org, and includes some great particularly upscale places like Erato, Atomic Cowboy, Café Napoli, and Lemongrass . . . if you feel like splurging, and you still haven't gotten the final bill from the hospital yet.

OHMYGOSH—I HAVE THE KID FOR THE DAY!

The little lady might not even want to leave the kid at all during this time, much less with you! But should she decide to get out of the house for a day of shopping, it's probably best to just stay home and catch up on your golf, fishing, NASCAR, or whatever else is on TV on Saturday afternoon.

Don't freak. Babies, like dogs and IRS agents, sense fear. Act confident even if you aren't.

If he starts to cry, ask yourself: Could he be hungry? Could he be sleepy? Is his diaper dirty? If it's "no" to these questions, he might just be missing the other parent—you know, the one with the breasts. Hold the baby and pace, and sing to him. Take him to the rocking chair . . . but don't panic, and for God's sake be a man and resist calling Mom about it.

In the worst cases, you'll have to be patient and let him cry it out.

Fun Fact!

Now that you have a baby, you can magically sing! Babies are like a really drunk crowd at a Helen Fitzgerald's karaoke night—they think ANYBODY can sing well. So here's your chance to be our town's next Nikko Smith!

And sure, Mom sings those boring lullabies, but you don't have to do that. A slow version of "For Those About to Rock (We Salute You)" or something by Chingy would work. Heck, he's a baby; he doesn't know the difference.

Chapter Two
Review Questions

1. In the hospital room, during delivery, you're as useful as . . .

    A. A designated hitter

    B. Golf on TV

    C. A third nipple

    D. A third male nipple

2. When in-laws become grandparents, it's . . .

    A. A promotion

    B. An excuse to ask *exactly* how much you make

    C. A boon to local retailers, especially Build-A-Bear

    D. Time to turn them into free babysitters

3. Complete this sentence: "For me, sleeping is . . .

    A. more important than life itself"

    B. overrated"

    C. something that parents in sitcoms do, but not something that happens in real life"

    D. something I'll get to later, like when I die"

4. True or False: "When women friends come over, I want to sit with them as they go over every detail of the birth, including the aroma and texture of the placenta."

5. Short Essay: Explain why on earth women with children *brag* about the size and length of their baby at birth, as if size matters or if it's some kind of bizarre contest. (Those able to do this with no sense of irony get an extra 10 points.)

When my oldest daughter, Ally, who is now 19, was six months old, I took charge of her for the whole day for the first time by myself. My wife was a little nervous about me doing this. She had pumped enough breast milk to feed the baby well into her thirties.

"I'm sure I can handle this," I said.

They're gonna put those words on my tombstone.

My wife left and I went in to check on little Ally. She was awake, so I put on white tights and a cute red jumper.

Then I dressed the baby.

That's a joke. Besides, I look puffy in red.

I changed her diaper. I got her dressed. I even brushed her strands of hair and scotch-taped a little bow to her head. Mostly I just looked at her; how tiny she was; how beautiful!

About 12:30 she got a little fussy, so I said, "All right, it's time for lunch." I warmed up a bottle, fed her half of it and then, unexplainably, her eyes rolled back into her head as if she was about to pass out.

I panicked. "Oh my God, she's dying! I'll be in so much trouble with your mother!" I cradled her in my right arm and paced the kitchen floor. I softly patted her butt, knowing I had to keep her from losing consciousness. I'd learned that from an episode of Mannix.

Finally, I called a neighbor who's a nurse. "The baby is dying!"

"Calm down, Craig. What's the problem?"

I said, "I don't know! Her eyes are rolling up in her head and she can't seem to stay awake."

"Has she had her nap?"

I hung up the phone. Yes, of course, her nap!

I took mine too.

—Craig Hawksley, comedian

CHAPTER THREE

MONTHS 3–6, AND HEY!
THERE'S A PERSON EMERGING
IN THAT POOPING, EATING,
SLEEPING MACHINE!

It's an exciting time as (hopefully) you'll start to come out of a sleep-deprived daze as the baby (hopefully, mostly) sleeps through the night (and by "night" we mean more than three hours at a time). Also, you'll secretly be pleased that at three months you haven't lost or broken the little thing. Whew!

A personality will start to emerge and reveal itself. You'll notice likes and dislikes, mood swings, and basic cable channel preferences. As the proverbial acorn doesn't fall too far from the tree, you'll notice similarities to the parents. There'll be lots of, "She has your eyes!" and "Look, he has your smile!" Hopefully, though, in the frustration that comes with being new parents, it won't degenerate into things like, "She stinks like you and needs a bath all the time," or "Look! He's got your tiny penis."

You will likely be tempted during this period to spend hours lying on the bed cooing and laughing with your baby. It's very un-guy-like, but give yourself permission to do it anyway.

PRIVATE BABY CONTRACTORS

You like it straight, so here it is: This is a tough, conflicted time. If you're really lucky, you're able to have Mom stay at home. No doubt about it, that is preferable for the baby and the family. There is nothing better for the child than a stay-at-home Mom . . . or Dad! Another option we want to toss out there is *you*, that's right, the Dad, staying at home with the kid. Believe it or not, this is a growing trend, as many dads are able to work part time or pretty close to full time out of their homes and/or as consultants. (For more on this, see Appendix A.)

Often, new parents are able to piece together some sort of arrangement involving Mom working part time, grandparents helping out a couple of days a week, and maybe a little day care. It's great if you can be creative and work something out.

But the economic reality for those whose last name isn't "Busch," "Chouteau," or "AmerenUE," is that both parents have to work. So if you haven't done it already, full-time day care for the baby will be happening at this point. Luckily, St. Louis is filled with quality, caring day care. It's a tough decision, of course, so get involved and help out. Visit these places with your wife and ask around about recommendations. Word of mouth is always the most helpful.

Location figures into the mix, too. Figure out who is dropping off and who is picking up, and what combination of both of your schedules can maximize your time with your baby.

DUDE, THE CHICK IS GOING TO CRY

Not counting your high school typing teacher, cyborgs, or perhaps one of the gals on the Archrival Rollergirls professional roller derby team, any woman who drops off the kid at day care is going to cry her eyes out. The pragmatic guy solution? YOU drop the kid off and have her pick him up. She'll still cry, but it'll be better. Really.

And speaking of her feelings . . . now you know how you're the problem solver? You're the pragmatic one? You're the justifier, explainer, big-picture machine? Well, if there's ever a time for you to turn all those faucets off and just "empathize" with the little lady, it's now. We know. There seems to be no point in talking about the situation again. You've already gone over all of this. But when she discusses how bad, guilty, etc., she feels about putting the kid into day care and going back to work, you'll WANT to say things like:

- "Well, we just have to do it. You can't quit your job."
- "She'll be fine—it's a real nice place."
- "There's worse things that could happen. Think if we had to put the baby in day care *and* we lived in Baghdad!"
- "The kid will turn out just fine. I went to day care, and look at me! Sure, a few arrests, but no convictions!"

Just listen to her and be supportive. Actually, you don't even really have to listen, just shut the hell up, which, if you're lucky, she'll interpret as listening.

How Soon Can I Have Sex?

Yes, we knew you were wondering when we'd get to this. Now, while the average St. Louis male thinks about sex every 7 seconds, during this very special time that number gets as high as 8.825 seconds.

Well, the great news is you can start having sex *immediately* after the baby is born! Just not with your wife. (Or with someone else—that would really be so uncool.)

If she had a relatively problem-free birth, sometime in the third to sixth month she might be ready. It's officially six weeks to "can"—*want* is a different story though, so definitely defer to her, as lots of things can get torn and sore during this whole crazy birth process. Some day in the future we'll figure out how to simply digitally download these baby things, but for now it's physically a pretty traumatic experience for the woman.

Also, patience is needed on how she looks. She's still a baby machine, and especially if she's breast-feeding, she's still be eating for two. So let's hold off on the not-too-subtle references, like how great Becky the Carpet Lady looks since she lost all that weight, and how relieved the flying carpet must be.

Psycho Mood Changes

Remember that really crazy girl you dated once, who at the flip of some mysterious switch could go from laughing to crying, sad to happy, angry to even angrier for seemingly no apparent reason?

What? You *married* her?

Oh. Well, good. Then you're prepared for Psycho Baby on Crack. Baby Claire can go from zero to stark raving screaming in 1.2 seconds during this

Fun Fact!

Babies are extremely talented at making bubbles with their saliva and making the raspberry sound. Here's your chance to return to your days on the kindergarten playground and do it right back at them! It's really a win-win situation.

period. Likely, this will rattle Mom, and that's why it's even more important for you to remain steadfast and calm.

Just as perplexing, or perhaps even more so, is going in the opposite direction. She'll first be screaming and then suddenly laughing and squealing. The changes are fast and swift, so buckle up.

BABY TALK

Now the baby is making lots of noises, and not just farting, which she does at impressively high volumes. And—shhhh!—she thinks she is talking. The vocabulary basically consists of:

- Aaaaaaaa
- Eeeeee
- Iiiiiiiiii
- Oooooooo
- Uuuuuuuu
- And sometimes yyyyyyyyyyy

Now Mom tends to talk to the kid a lot, and it's a good idea for you to do it as well. There's no reason to start full-blown conversations with the little gal at this point. But she can't talk back, you say?

EXACTLY.

It's a great idea to take advantage of this, as when the kid is 7 or 12 or 16 or 35, she might not care what the heck you have to say. So when the baby looks at you and suddenly goes . . .

BABY: Aaaaaaaaaagh.

DAD: Well, I'm glad you asked. See, when choosing a compound miter saw, first ask yourself, "What are my short term needs?"

BABY: IiiiiiiiiiiOOOOOOOaaaag.

DAD: Exactly! For example, what do you want to work on first?

BABY: OOOOoooooooEEEEEEEaaaaaaa . . .

DAD: A new deck with built-in hot tub. I like the way you think!

BABY: Aah! Aah! Aah!

DAD: Exactly—something we can all enjoy. So you'll want something about 2,000 watts of power and a pivoting fence for cutting crown molding . . .

BABY: [huge fraternity-size fart]

DAD: Well, one with a laser marker sounds a bit extravagant, but what the heck! We deserve it!

MUSIC

Now there's an entire industry based on this whole "Baby Mozart" craze, where by listening to classical music, the kid becomes the next Einstein or John Danforth or something.

And thus many well-meaning friends will provide you with classical music. However, while it's debatable whether it makes little Albert smarter or not, having that music on in the house certainly makes things *calmer*, which is pretty important to the new Dad, Mom, and said baby.

So hopefully you won't get any opera, and if you do, feel free to hate the person who gave it to you. Mozart and Bach instrumentals, particularly the piano and harpsichord, work. But what is really nice for all is solo classical guitar music—anything from John Williams, Christopher Parkening, or Pepe Romero is a great choice.

Any basic cable plan from Charter Cable features great music stations with no commercials, and their "light classical" station is great to have on in the background. And if you are one of those closet John Tesh fans, their "soundscapes" has calming new-age music. DirectTV satellite also offers great music stations, but they're not available with all their packages.

So flip that on, and then you can walk around with your iPod blaring Nelly.

ANIMAL DEMOTIONS

Just as your parents and the in-laws got promoted in this restructuring of Your Home, Inc., those of the four-legged variety who drink from bowls from the floor are going to be inadvertently knocked down a peg or three. This will be a hard adjustment for Fido and Princess, but most of the time they will figure out that the new thing that sometimes wiggles around on the floor is not a new stuffed toy for them.

Occasionally, there is a problem. The pets get so jealous that they are aggressive around the baby. If they ever do anything to harm the baby, tough decisions have to be made, and because of your wife's delicate condition, you'll need to make them.

Most of the time, they adjust—and so do you, as 99 percent of the walking, feeding, playing, and joyous kitty-litter scooping will fall solely on you. So if you only tolerated her annoying Siamese cats before, now those images of "accidentally" leaving them in the freezer move from mere fantasy to full-blown premeditation.

Otherwise, you might find the pets looking sadly at you, trying to make you feel guilty for taking care of the baby instead of petting them. Just remind them that at least they are able to lick themselves, and that should make them feel better.

Is There Nothing This Thing Won't Put in His Mouth?

No. Many so-called "specialists" will tell you it's his way of "exploring the world." However, at the Youth University of Children and Kids (YUCK), located in an old tent behind the especially large dumpster in Dogtown, studies have revealed that babies like doing this for the sheer joy of seeing Mom and Dad completely grossed out. It's an early power play, and very effective.

"Ideally," you will always monitor what the baby puts in his mouth, and he will always be supervised while on a freshly washed blanket on the vacuumed floor with lots of appropriate, sterilized, brightly colored baby toys. And by "ideally" we mean just as ideally the work on Highway 40 will be completed early and under budget.

Yes, your definition of what is "clean" will radically change during this period. You can either completely freak out and try to create a hygienic environment suitable for lab work, or when the baby rolls over and grabs the dog's squeaky toy and thrusts it into his mouth, simply stay seated in your recliner and rationalize, "It's building up his immune system."

Hopefully you'll end up somewhere in between and not lose your mind or your lunch.

GUY OUTFITS VS. UNFRIENDLY GUY OUTFITS

As you'll figure out, everything is "cute" about a baby—spoon, clothes, snot—because it's "tiny" . . . as in, "Look at these little itty bitty shoes—aren't they cute?" Aside from the "My Dad Can Kick Your Dad's Ass" shirt you bought him, you'll be mostly unimpressed and wonder how something that small can cost $32.95.

But should she dress the baby for a situation when you're going to be in charge, absolutely do not let her dress the thing in those "onesies"—they are incredibly annoying and very un-guy-friendly. You'll wonder what the point is of having something that wraps around and even snaps down there, yet is also a shirt. Who makes up this stuff? Make sure the baby is in your basic pants and shirt combo, because if changing the baby is a bit of a drag to begin with, those things are a total drag.

Mirrors and Other Babies

Like an Ursuline prom queen or a star runner on Vianney's track team, your little Albert or Claire loves to revel in his or her own image. Take advantage of this in a Dad-manageable activity when, say, the baby is thrust in your face by a disgruntled, shower-deprived Mom who then disappears into the bathroom for what seems like days: mirror play.

Ideally, you have a floor-length mirror in the house, but standing at your dresser in front of the

Fun Fact!

Besides humans, chimps are the only mammals on the planet who can identify themselves in a mirror! Should your baby not be able to recognize his or her image, please check with the hospital. You might have accidentally brought home an orangutan.

While it might not seem worth it, kids this age actually enjoy getting together with other babies. Babies as young as six weeks old are able to develop social relationships with other infants and toddlers. Also, it's a nice break for the parents in that it counts as social interaction too.

wall mirror also works. Interact by asking questions: "Who is the baby? Who is the baby?" Then give lots of approval when they figure it out. Next, there's "Who is the daddy?"

Hopefully, you'll be able to identify the two.

Obviously, you can enjoy a libation and conversation yourself—just don't take your eyes off the babies, of course, lest they sneak out behind the barn for their first cigarette.

WHERE TO TAKE A 3-6 MONTH OLD

You can still likely take the baby anywhere, if you're keyed into his schedule. Honestly, it might be the last chance for you to get out to that nicer restaurant—assuming you can time it to happen when he's sleeping.

Try, because, alas, you are now at the vestibule of what is known as the "no restaurant zone." So just understand that if you are in a nicer restaurant, you have to be a man and take the kid outside if he starts screaming. Be respectful of the others trying to have a nice meal. And for some reason, it's the Dad's job to do this while the Mom finishes her meal. We think it's because guys eat notoriously faster.

Otherwise, avoid excessively loud places like the bowling alley, the casino, and the Edward Jones Dome. Probably best to avoid your cousin's trailer in Hillsboro, too.

Ohmygosh—I Have the Kid
for the Day!

You might be tempted to just stay home, but we believe you're ready to take the baby out. You've probably noticed how he loves a change of environment, so it's really win-win to go on errands like running to Target, going to the coffee shop, having a nice lunch at a tavern—or even just going to the park.

It's true, he's not too young to be taken to a playground, ideally one of the smaller ones that are around town. Take a book or magazine. Set the kid down in the shade where he can watch the other kids play and relax! (Relax as in relax with one eye on the baby at all times.)

Didja Know?

Should you be out and have forgotten something like a diaper or, worse, the whole damn diaper bag, playing the "dumb dad" routine will get you far. Just zero in on another Mom with a similarly aged kid, shuffle up to her and explain the situation, do an aw-shucks and roll your eyes, and . . . poof! Free diaper.

But for God's sake, don't forget the diaper bag, and make sure the diaper bag is stocked properly with:

- Diapers (obviously)
- Moist wipes (very important)
- At least two changes of clothes (for the baby, not for you—though an extra T-shirt for you when he spits up isn't a bad idea)
- Book or magazine
- Bottle for baby

CHAPTER THREE
REVIEW QUESTIONS

1. When shopping for proper day care, you'll want to make sure:

    A. The sitter doesn't have the TV on all day

    B. The place is relatively clean and has plenty of toys

    C. The sitter is not a Cubs fan

    D. All of the above

2. The baby's first sounds will likely be:

    A. Vowel sounds

    B. Some "colorful phrase" you uttered every time he spit up on you

    C. "He shoots, he scores!"

    D. In French

3. If you have a dog, the dog will:

    A. Ask you to exchange the baby for a squirrel—something he can chase

    B. Resent the lack of attention, but take the opportunity to lick the baby's spit-up off the floor as a consolation prize

    C. Constantly tell the cat, "Well, at least I'm not a cat!"

    D. Bark in French

4. True or False: It's okay if the baby gets into the litter box.

5. Short Essay: Explain why it's good to have nonsensical conversations with your baby but not so much with a Hazelwood police officer.

When he was a young man, he would dress a certain way or behave in a particular manner. I would say to him, "They don't dress that way, or they don't act like that." He would look up to me and say, "Dad, who are they?" He was always determined to do things the right way, no matter what I thought or what anybody else thought.

—Francis R. Slay, about his son, St. Louis City Mayor, Francis G. Slay

CHAPTER FOUR

MONTHS **6–12**, AND WHY CRAWLING IS CUTE UNTIL THEY ACTUALLY DO IT

Remember when your college roommate, Russell, got so drunk all he could do was roll around on the floor? And you thought that was pathetic?

Well, when your baby does it for the first time, it's the coolest thing in the world. And just like Russell, he'll likely need to be changed after. But you won't mind doing it in this case.

It's a very exciting time when the baby starts moving—right up to and excluding the moment she *really* starts moving. First she will roll over. Then she will roll *over there*—right by the light socket you never plugged up or by the basement door that you now have to remember to always shut.

Then there is the "army crawl," in which she channels the spirit of old World War II movies and digs her elbows into the floor as if enemy fire is buzzing over her head. Sometimes, but not always, she'll skip this and go straight to the basic crawl. Or she'll be a "scootcher," which can only be described as crawling while still sitting. Regardless of which way she does it, and definitely regardless of how many cute toys she has that go *buzz! whirl! wee!* that cost $42.73 at Toys "R" Us, she'll be scoping out the dog dish.

And you don't even have a dog. That's how determined babies are in going for the things you don't want them to go for.

She'll win this one.

CRUISING

Then, just when you start getting used to the crawling, she will pull herself up on chairs, coffee tables, and bookshelves and start moving around this way. This, oddly enough, is called "cruising,"

Didja Know?

Your floor is totally disgusting, and you live like rats in a sewage plant!

Not really, but it'll suddenly seem like that, especially to Mom, once the precious fruit of your loins starts rolling around with the dust bunnies, chip crumbs, and bottle caps of days gone by. Mom will want to sterilize the place. You'll want to form a committee to redefine what "clean" is. She'll want you to pick up after yourself, *really I mean it this time.* You'll want to muse that a wide variety of found objects, not just toys made by "real toy makers," are intellectually stimulating.

---

which is something you associate with teenage boys driving to the various McDonald's in South County on a Friday night.

This is much cuter to watch in action, but alas, just as dangerous. Just when you got comfortable with what was on the ground, now you have to re-evaluate everything that is at the two-foot level.

Babies are extremely fast creatures and can go from zero to oh-crap-don't-touch-my-stereo-receiver in 4.3 seconds! Of course, they never do this when you're looking at them. They do it when you step out of the room for just a moment . . .

BE A MAN—LET IT GO

You know those floor-based CD stands with your hundreds of CDs categorized, alphabetized, and color coordinated? Gone. Don't even try to prolong it, because your Wilco through your Zappa CDs will be pulled out of the bottom of your rack, opened up, and grubbed up beyond use. This is tough because you just trained your wife in the subtle nuances of your system (you know, before she rolled her eyes, muttered, "Yeah, whatever," and went back to listening to her old Wham! cassettes). Now you have this creature maniacally working his way through your collection. . . .

Don't fight it. The first time it happens, pick your favorite 50, put them high on a bookshelf, and box the rest of them up for a year or so.

The Precious Remote Controls

As we've established, crawling and cruising babies have all the toys in the world, but what they instinctively want is your glass of beer, your bowl of corn chips, and, most of all, your remotes.

Yes, your days of leaving the remote on the coffee table are gone, gone, gone. At the Technological University of Beer & Entertainment (TUBE), located in a bunker under a strip mall in Arnold, scientists and unemployed plumbers have been working on this issue. After extensive clinical trials, they have come to recommend that new dads adapt an early aggressive Remote Retention Plan (RRP).

Believe us, a strong RRP is crucial to your mental well-being. If necessary, you can call in one of TUBE's highly qualified consultants (his name is Eugene), but most likely you can save yourself the $2.72 and simply sit down with your wife and figure out where these important "tools of life" are going to be placed. Your typical RRP program might be, "Always leave the remotes on top of the TV" or "placed on the bookshelf between your copy of *Diehard Card: St. Louis Cardinals 2006 World Series Champions* and *Beyond Toasted Ravioli: A Tour of St. Louis Restaurants.*"

TUBE warns that those who neglect to develop an RRP risk catastrophic situations, such as when your wife is upstairs giving the kid a bath and *24* is about to come on and you're tearing up the house looking for the damn remote.

Odd Sounds

At some point during this period, there is a very good chance that Albert or Claire will discover the vocal chords, and he or she will become particularly fond of a certain sound that will, naturally, be the most grating and annoying sound the little creature could possibly settle on. This will become "the sound." It might be an extremely high-pitched screech. It might remind one of the sounds that came out of Peter Boyle as the dancing monster in *Young Frankenstein.* It'll be loud, and it'll be annoying, and call it number 973 on the list of things you can't control and must live with.

You might want to make the sound right back at the baby, but that will only encourage him. Try making more pleasant, calm, quiet sounds like, "goo," "ga," and "shhhhh—the news is on."

Little Frickin' Isaac Newton

Babies will discover gravity, and you'll discover your back has never quite recovered from high school football. Yes, little Albert will be dropping something all the time, and it'll be months, even years, before he figures out why it doesn't just hover where he lets go of it.

You'll find this cute for about, oh, 3.2 seconds. And that's if you're patient. So when you start to move him into the high chair, it'll be pretty tempting to tie everything to his wrist. But this is not recommended as it can escalate to tethering him to things like couches later, which unfortunately is not cool anymore.

First Words

There's a very good chance you'll hear little Claire utter her first word during this period. It would be *just really so* great if it's not of the kind that needed to be bleeped out when *The Sopranos* went into reruns on basic cable.

You can spin this any way you want, but assuming you're not cursing like a sailor around

Didja Know?

You're HILARIOUS to kids this age! You're a regular Robin Williams. Enjoy getting big laughs from your baby by your pretend-to-sneeze routine, your popping your cheeks . . . and remember that killer fart sound you used to make with your hand and armpit? How it somehow fell out of fashion shortly after high school? Well, great news: Drag it out and dust it off, because it KILLS now! You'll get huge laughs with it.

your house, the great news is the baby's first word will very likely be "da–da." Now the fact is, it's easier for her to say "da–da" than "ma–ma." But sure, tell your spouse that you read somewhere that the baby's first words correspond with whom she thinks is the best dressed.

Now, everyone is on their own timetable, so don't freak out if this doesn't happen by the first birthday. The first words usually come between twelve and fifteen months. Then of course, the subject immediately turns to the weather.

PARALLEL TALK

Your wife will get this from one of those huge baby books, but one extremely important aspect of language development is parallel talk. Get in the habit of labeling what the baby is doing. It's important that you participate in this process with the mom, not only to offer extra reinforcement in the development of language, but also to stake out your role as a teacher.

So when you're watching him interact with anything, name it: "Albert looking at book?" "Albert playing with rattle?" "Albert opening daddy's gun rack and getting out daddy's deer rifle?"

Point to objects and identify them for him. "This is a chair. We sit in chair!"

Exaggerate your excitement for this kind of activity—pretend you're talking about the upcoming tailgate party. Being really excited in voice inflections and in facial expressions about that chair, and being unusually thrilled that we sit in that chair, helps greatly with a baby's language development. You want your baby to have good language skills . . . right up to the time he's sixteen and tells you he hates you because all of his friends have microchips implanted in their brains, which is needed for the latest version of Playstation, so why can't he?

Then you might regret the whole language-development thing. But don't think about that now.

Long Distance Travel

There might come a point where you have to go far away to take said baby somewhere to show him off. You might have relatives in some other part of the country; you might be on the lam because of that string of robberies at Dirt Cheap Cigarettes stores. Either way, if there's any way to drive there, do it. Plan plenty of breaks, and try to drive through the night if at all possible.

If you have to take the baby on a plane, be prepared for an extremely taxing trip. You won't "have" to buy a seat for a baby that is under two years old, though if you happen to be one of the Roberts brothers, do. It'll make everything easier.

When you have to travel on a plane, you have to bring a ton of crap. The car seat. The stroller. The amazing amount of clothes babies go through in a simple five-day period. Plus, wherever you're going, they are going to load you up with baby crap to take back with you. So here are the travel tips:

- **Pack Extremely Lightly for Yourself.** You lived in one pair of jeans for weeks at a time in college. Now is the time to revisit that experience.
- **Do You Really Need It?** Stand over your wife as she packs and ask her if she needs absolutely everything. That precious baby blanket? Well, they have a bath towel where you're going and that'll work just fine.
- **Creature Comforts? Ha!** You know how you like to walk on the plane with your big cup of Starbucks, your copy of *St. Louis Magazine*, your laptop with DVDs, and your iPod? Fuhgettaboutit. You and your wife will be in full baby control and it'll be all about keeping your hands free and carrying as few objects as possible.
- **Friendly Skies? Ha! Ha!** The baby will scream and cry, and you will think you smell burning hair as the glares of other passengers bore into the back of your head. Relax. It's not as bad for them as you think it is. And if it is, let it go. (And next time you fly alone on business, be generous with a reassuring smile to the couple-with-the-screaming-baby yourself. You know, before you see if you have enough miles to be bumped up to first class.)
- **Pre-emptive Strike.** It might seem rude for the typical St. Louis guy, but consider being firm and clear to your hosts about baby gifts. Obviously, Aunt Rombauer will want to buy that huge baby tilt-a-whirl that can't fit in the trunk of a '72 Ford LTD, but gently encourage her to give something like a single outfit instead—something that you can use at your destination, thus making one less thing to pack.

Get to Lambert at least 90 minutes before the flight, too, as no doubt you'll be departing from terminal 274 and have to walk an extra three miles carrying everything. Once at the gate, let the baby crawl around a bit. Sure, it's a tad unsavory, but he's about to be held tightly for a long flight to Miami.

Finally, consider getting on the plane at the last possible minute. Sometimes they let families with infants board early, but this makes no sense—once you're in those seats you're stuck for two, three, four or more hours. Why prolong the agony?

Didja Know?

Flying with a baby during the holidays, like Christmas and Thanksgiving, *sucks*. Try to use the common sense God gave you to tell your wife and distant-living family members that the baby doesn't know what day it is. Celebrate the holiday a week later or earlier, and fly when it's cheaper and easier. You will make great sense before you are unceremoniously overruled.

ENJOY IT

By now, calmness should be prevailing for both you and Mom. It should be kicking in—*wow, I'm a dad. I'm not going to break the baby. I know how to change diapers. I can wipe a snotty nose with the best of them!*

It's a great feeling, and it gets better with quality time. Spend time on the floor, stacking up blocks for her to knock down. Lie on your back and let her crawl over you. Be physical with her, and let her see affection between you and the missus (nothing too graphic of course—don't want her in therapy the rest of her life . . . just hand-holding and kisses.)

If you're stressed out at work, it's easy to just sit and be in the room with the kid because the baby at this age doesn't demand much from you other than to make sure she doesn't kill herself. But if you can, spend some time on the floor engaging the child as much as possible. Zone out *after* she goes to bed.

Fun Fact!

Babies are a BABE MAGNET. As you'll quickly discover, lots of people want to comment on how cute your baby is, and a guy with a baby is somehow very cool. So share the wealth! Clark, your lame-ass, still-single high school buddy, the one who is always complaining about not meeting chicks? Give him a crash course in Baby Maintenance and send him to the mall with baby. When women coo over the baby, he'll get to say he's just helping out a friend, and he'll look especially attractive, despite his rumpled appearance.

WHERE TO TAKE A
6-12 MONTH OLD

If it's winter, there's nothing like a stroll around the mall to break up the tedium. Most of the area malls offer the fun little car strollers and, of course, lots of people and bright lights to look at. Several of the Westfield malls, like West County, South County, and the nearly dead Crestwood, have little playgrounds where, if they aren't too crowded, are great for kids this age to crawl around. St. Louis Mills in Hazelwood is huge and also has an indoor playground for bigger kids. This definitely requires close monitoring, however, as sometimes these things can turn into a World Wrestling Federation event.

If it's not cold out, you can take babies pretty much anywhere. Everything is an adventure with lots to look at, so take them to the hardware store, the Office Depot, heck, even the DMV! (Though don't let them on the floor—those places are gross.) It's a good bonding experience and makes running simple errands fun for you.

OHMYGOSH—I HAVE THE KID FOR THE DAY!

If it's a beautiful day, not too hot, not too cold (you know, the three days of spring and two and a half days in the fall when that happens in St. Louis), pack up the baby and take her into the world of visual stimulation, like our superb Forest Park, someplace many of us don't go to enough. It's such a huge park, and the walking paths are easy to negotiate. You get out and stretch your legs, too, and it all makes for a little father/baby bonding. Take her after her nap, of course.

Too cold? When was the last time you were at the Art Museum or the History Museum? Again, great places to stroll around, with lots to look at. After any of the above, treat yourselves to lunch in U. City at Fitz's. Man, is there a lot to look at there, especially if you get a spot by the bottling windows.

CHAPTER FOUR
REVIEW QUESTIONS

1. Your college roommate, Russell, and your baby, have the following characteristics in common (check all that apply):

    A. Drool

    B. Roll around on the floor

    C. Always pick up the check at Fast Eddie's

    D. Need to be reminded that it's not always about them

2. The baby's ability to disrupt your regular routine sinks in, and appropriate behavior modifications are necessary and reasonable. Which of the following is *not* appropriate?

    A. Putting away your CDs

    B. Keeping your remotes off the coffee table

    C. Moving to Guam

    D. Letting the baby crawl around the DMV

3. Flying with a baby is most like . . .

    A. . . . a bike ride on the Katy Trail with friends

    B. . . . a fall afternoon at the Villa Antonio Winery in Hillsboro

    C. . . . being locked in the coat closet at Rigazzi's on a Saturday night

    D. . . . bungee-jumping while holding your wife's cat, Engelbreit

4. True or False: It's easier for you to "parallel talk" with your baby than for your wife to parallel park in Soulard during Mardi Gras.

5. Short Essay: Your baby said his first word, and it's something you typically yell at the TV when the Rams are down more than 14 points at the half. Explain your way out of this in 250 words or less.

As a young girl, my daughter Michelle decided to run away. She left a note for my wife and me telling us where she'd be. When I came home from work, I asked my wife if she'd picked up Michelle. She said no, and I asked why. She said Michelle had run off to a family that had six kids. "When they start to fix dinner," my wife said, "they'll bring her home." And that's exactly what happened.

—Retired U.S. Congressman William L. Clay, Sr.

Chapter Five

Months 12–18, and the Joy, Nay the Necessity, of Takeout

You won't remember exactly when it'll happen, but you'll be out to dinner, and you'll have just had to change a diaper-most-foul on the men's room sink *just* as your dinner is served. When you make it back to the table, your beer will be flat, the dinner will be cold, and the kid will be shrieking.

You'll think: "How did I get here?"

Yes, while you'd always figured places like 1111 Mississippi, Tony's, and Sydney Street Cafe were off the list, you'll eventually come to the horrifying realization that even Hodak's, Growler's, and the Pasta House are out.

Welcome to the world of takeout, because suddenly eating out, almost *any* eating out, is so fraught with stress and danger that it ceases to be worth it. It might be depressing, but buck up and accept it. You'll be better off succumbing to this situation than fighting it, and just remind yourself it's only for a year (or five or ten—depending on how many kids you have).

Not that we're bashing any of St. Louis's great independent restaurants, but they tend to be great because of their relaxing atmospheres. If you really need a decent meal out, your chain restaurants— Macaroni Grills, Olive Gardens, Houlihan's—are actually very child-friendly and built on (usually) lightning-fast service. They are designed to be all about turning tables quickly, and if you're feeling as lucky as a Powerball winner, you can get in and out of those places fast.

But no matter what your restaurant of choice is, *go early*. If you're not in the car heading out by 5:05 at the extreme latest, the odds of it being a nightmare experience ending in excessive doggie bags are higher than the Arch.

For reasons too complex to fully comprehend, *you* will always be the one who has to go out and get the food (we think it goes back to the dawn of

That restaurant hostess giving you that *look*, the one with the raised eyebrow? She's wondering if you're just glad to see her or if there's something in your pocket. Alas, it's the latter, because without realizing it, you've gotten into the habit of going to a restaurant with several Hot Wheels or a Barbie doll shoved into your jeans pocket creating an, er, bulge. Damn—if you had only thought of that trick when you were single!

---

humankind—you know, that whole hunter-gatherer thing). So get acquainted with all of the restaurants nearby and start collecting takeout menus. Go ahead and try the nicer restaurants—some, like the Great Restaurants (Blue Water Grill, Remy's, Big Sky) are good at preparing takeout; others aren't because they are just not set up that way. Places like Gourmet to Go (www.gourmet-to-go.com) and Art of Entertaining are also good (www.theaofe.com) if you're in an upscale mood. But bring something home from one of the nicer places once in a while, as it'll offer a hint of civility to your lives that you'll both appreciate.

One more tip: On that Friday night, after a long week of work, when you're staring at a weekend in, don't call the order in. Insist to her that you go there and order it at the bar so you can bring it home exactly the moment it's ready, and then . . . Hey! Look! You're at a bar, a man among men! As you give your order to the tender, throw in a Jack and Coke (with a lime) or a big glass of Schlafly Pale and enjoy 15–20 minutes of adult time.

Yet, one more tip: An alternative to carryout is Time for Dinner (timefordinner.com) or Super Suppers, which are essentially prep kitchens where customers prepare a dozen or so meals to freeze for later use. Customers are forced to wear an apron, so at all costs don't go, unless you're into that sort of thing. These places allow groups of women to share bottles of wine together while they prepare a meal, so you can pitch it to your wife and friends as a night out. Then have the guys over for a poker game.

FAVORITE PART OF THE BABY MONITOR

One of the tools of the trade is the baby monitor, and you're going to want to get a good one. It's a microphone that allows you to hear what is going on in the baby room or anywhere in the house. Since it's one way, baby can't hear you.

Say Mom goes out for the day, and you put the baby down. You simply call some of your buddies over, pop open some brewskis, and watch the game.

The better monitors also have a light meter to *show* you when the baby is starting to make noise in case the game gets so loud you can't hear.

Eventually, the baby will stir. You'll hear some movement, maybe some clanging of the crib. Now, your wife would jump up at this point, but not you! You hang. Next you'll hear the kiddo making some noises, maybe even "da da, da da da da da." Now you'll consider going up, but the Rams special teams just took the kickoff all the way to the 47, and how often does that happen? Stay and watch the replay, and then see if they can move the ball down the field.

Eventually, the baby will start full-blown screaming. She'll be screaming so loudly that you can almost hear without the monitor. The lights on the top of the meter will be flashing like a cop car. *Then* you'll know to act. You'll lean over, simply turn *off* the baby monitor, and then maybe turn the TV up a little louder.

The off switch. That's the best part of the baby monitor!

WHY THEY CALL IT "TODDLING"

It's been said about kids this age that they are like little drunks. They are really happy one moment. Then they fall down. Then they cry really hard. Then they just want to hug. Then they start laughing hysterically—all in the span of a minute. Despite recognizing this behavior from personal experience, this is *not* the time for you to share *your* tales of getting drunk, emotional, and falling down. Save that for a little later—like when they are forty-two.

Toddling aptly describes their mode of transportation: It's the time when they are able to pull themselves up on the coffee table and other low-to-the-ground objects like the couch, waddle a bit, and fall down. In fact, most of all, fall down. Lots and lots and lots of falling down.

As you know all too well, falling down is part of life. With your firstborn, it's easy to overreact and try to "save" him every time he falls on his butt. There will be times when he smashes his little head against a table leg, hard, and then you remember that it's *your baby* doing this, and you're not watching a Three Stooges movie. Pointing and laughing? Not so appropriate.

But neither is jumping to his "rescue" every single time. This is all part of the learning process, and this is just one of the many times you'll get to utter something like, "It's a hard-knock life, kid; better get used to it!"

BATH TIME

A duty that often gets completely delegated to the Mom is bath time. It's a shame, because it's a great time for Dad to interact with baby (also a great time for Dad to get as soaked as a ride on the log flume at Six Flags). Sometimes you'll hear of dads getting in the bathtub with the baby. Your instincts will tell you that that's kinda weird, if not downright awkward.

Go with your instincts.

But giving Mom some time to herself or a break from this routine is a great idea for both of you. Lest she be against the idea because you won't do as "good" a job as she does, be like, "Um, duh, I'm a guy, of course I won't." But that's not the point.

Go crazy with the bubble bath, put on a water puppet show with the bath toys, and for goodness sake, do your best getting into those cracks and crevices. Most of all, enjoy this great bonding time. (This is also a great time to think, "Hey, when was the last time I washed *my* cracks and crevices?")

DIDJA KNOW?

Everything you like to watch on TV is suddenly too offensive to have on while you-know-who is in the room.

From here on, until, like, they are in college, prepare to be guilt-tripped into not watching war movies, HBO shows, or even (gulp) the *Simpsons.* Find a refuge in the house with another TV, or you will be stuck watching *House Calls with Dr. Valerie Walker* and *Antiques Roadshow* on Channel 9 for at least the next decade.

MAKE EVERYTHING FUN

While your mind might be a million miles away on work, or you're just zoning out, or let's be honest, you're maybe a teensy-weensy resentful that you're having to change that diaper, no need to inadvertently take it out on her and do it in resolved silence. Play, talk, and/or sing to her. Make everything fun—it's all in your tone. So as long as you can say it with a big smile and the voice inflection normally reserved for use by Channel 4's Vickie Newton reporting a cute puppy lost-then-found story, you can be like "Yes! And *then* do you know what happened? Daddy's big stinking head-up-his-butt boss declared that the sales projection figures weren't detailed enough even though he only had two hours on a Friday afternoon to put them together, and now Daddy has to spend Saturday in Excel hell! Yes! Daddy does!"

Because of his unusual occupation and the evening hours he worked, local comedian Craig Hawksley was a stay-at-home dad for his three daughters, and he will proudly tell you that he changed diapers every day for nine years. That would demoralize a lesser man, to be sure, but, of course, Hawksley had fun with it. He says he would use the opportunity to work on his sportscaster impression and give a play-by-play of the task at hand: *"Yes, he steps up to the plate . . . reaches down and takes off the pants . . . swing and miss! I tell ya Bob, who knows where this is going . . . there he is again, taking aim at removing the diaper and . . . oh! It's a doozy! Look at that, it's out of the ballpark, quality-poop wise! The fans are going wild! It's a winner!"*

All to the squealing delight of his daughters.

Entertaining the kid on the changing table has a practical angle, especially as he gets bigger. If you're doing it silently, he will quickly get bored and start moving and wiggling, making the not-terribly-pleasant job harder and more time consuming. Keep 'em laughing, and you'll be done quicker!

FUNNY SOUNDS

This is a tough one, as it's something that doesn't come naturally to a guy, but it's important that both parents participate as much as possible in the baby's development. As he explores his vocal cords, extremely odd sounds will come out. Get right in there and show him what makin' odd sounds is *really* all about. After all, as Mom will surely attest, no one can do it like you.

No one is looking, so jump right in and make funny sounds back at him, like raspberries, etc. The finger-popping-of-the-cheeks is always a showstopper. Also: Get in the habit of imitating his weird vocal renderings, scat-like singing, and channeling of a Cahokia tribal chieftain after having stepped into an ornately weaved basket full of copperhead snakes. And when you master his sounds, try them out in the boardroom!

Fun Fact!

Your toddler will likely be growing increasingly curious about your food. Use sound judgment of what to "share" with him (Einstein's bagel), what to let him have a small part of (Ted Drewes concrete), and what to put in a blender and puree for him (Growler's hot buffalo wings). Then again, maybe wait before you start putting wings in the blender.

MOM AND DAD TIME

You know how when you're on an airplane, and the flight attendants are telling you what to do in case of emergency? (Yes, we ignore them, too.) But take our word for it when we recall that when the air masks pop down, if you're with a small child, you are to put yours on *first*, then put the child's on.

Why? Because if you are not fully functioning, you are not going to be of much help to the child.

With this in mind, it's time for you and Mom to start forging a little adult time. Yes, you spend countless evenings "together" collapsed on the couch watching some movie from Netflix or just flipping through the channels while she goes in and out of consciousness, but that's not what we're talking about. It's time to arrange for a babysitter and get out, just the two of you, to at least a nice meal, if not a full-blown rowdy night that ends at the Big Bang on Laclede's Landing belting out Neil Diamond songs with the rest of the crowd.

Ironically, you'll find yourself mostly talking about the baby, but that's okay. Some semblance of your former life will go a long way in refueling your batteries.

The hardest part is you have to take charge and make a conscious effort to make it happen. Thoughtful planning, sometimes weeks in advance, is necessary because realizing on Saturday afternoon that it would be fun to hit Westport Plaza that evening is generally not going to cut it.

OUR GREAT OUTDOORS

As you may or may not recall from high school science class, observation is the most fundamental part of the scientific process. Your little Albert or Alberta Einstein needs to see things for him- or herself and, weather permitting (and even when it's not that hospitable), taking toddlers outside is one of the best things you can do for them.

You'll notice those fancy three-wheel all-terrain strollers that allow parents to run while the world is just a blur for the kid. Of course, those workout things are fine—for *you*.

But leisurely walks in your neighborhood, parks, and great places like Powder Valley, Faust Park, or Illinois's Pere Marquette State Park, are better because you can interact better with your child. Point to things you see and name them: "Look over there, a doggie!" "Look at the red birdie in the tree. Does Albert see the red birdie in the tree?" and "Lookie—Mrs. McGillicuddy is wandering around outside in just her housecoat and no underwear again—can you say 'underwear'?" It doesn't have to be a nonstop talk-fest, but don't just walk in silence plugged into your iPod, either.

Picnics are great for the whole family at this time; hit your local park and lay down your blanket in view of the playground, as he'll love watching the bigger kids play. Also, while the missus will tend to "freak out" about him crawling/rolling off the blanket, it's an important part of exploring. Let him touch, feel, even put a stick in his mouth. Draw the line at broken glass and hypodermic needles, but as long as he's under your moderately watchful eye, it's all part of his development. And who knows, maybe he'll grow up and be better at science than you! (And yeah, that is one bar that is set a little low. . . .)

WHERE TO TAKE A 12–18 MONTH OLD

The problem at this age is she basically wants to get down and walk as much as possible, capable of creating Godzilla-like havoc wherever she goes. Restaurants beyond McDonald's generally rely on a "Do you feel lucky?" mood, and if your timing is perfect and stars are aligned (and you get a booth), your local tavern for a beer and a burger is doable.

Otherwise it's running errands that aren't too long, parks, and the zoo.

OH MY GOSH—I HAVE THE KID FOR THE DAY!

One of St. Louis's many treasures is Grant's Farm. "Free" (except the eight dollars it costs to park), it's perfect for a dad/toddler experience. The forty-five-minute animal shows might not keep a young child's attention, but she'll love to watch the older kids feed the goats (don't let her in the cage though, she's too young—those little guys get pretty aggressive). The farm's small enough that she can waddle around, or splurge for one of the cool carriages for her to ride in. The side bonus is there are the two free beers waiting for you at the end of it. If the weather's bad, the Saint Louis Science Center is a great place to toddle around and catch an eyeful. With either of these, though, you'll be glad you got there early, pretty much exactly when they open, to avoid the heavy crowds.

CHAPTER FIVE
REVIEW QUESTIONS

1. When ordering takeout from a nicer restaurant, it's probably a bad idea to order the . . .

    A. Prosciutto-wrapped scallops

    B. Wild mushroom & escargot puff pastry

    C. Sushi on a stick

    D. Those dishes the waiter has to set on fire at your table before serving them

2. Toddling is to walking, what . . .

    A. Hiking is to Bicycling

    B. The Tower Tee Golf Course is to the St. Louis Country Club Course

    C. J-Kwon is to Nelly

    D. The *Riverfront Times* is to Something Someone Would Actually Read

3. Which one of these TV shows should you probably not have on when your toddler is in the room?

    A. *The Sopranos*

    B. *Barney*

    C. Barney guest starring on an episode of *The Sopranos* in which he gets whacked by Silvio behind the Bada Bing! Club

    D. The Weather Channel

4. If a toddler is at full toddle speed and is at one end of the 20' × 10' room and is heading toward a pair of scissors, a can of turpentine, and a rare Ming vase from the sixteenth century that was accidentally left on the floor at the opposite end of the room, and you jump from your chair and run to catch the toddler, achieving a speed of 4.2 miles an hour, the toddler will:

> A. Beat you to all three
>
> B. Only get to the Ming vase and break it in a million pieces
>
> C. Fall down and start crying
>
> D. Fake you out, make a left into the kitchen at the last minute, and start playing with that pile of explosives your wife accidentally left by the dog dish

5. Because simulating fart sounds will trigger squeals of delight from your toddler, list at least 215 ways this can be done. You have three minutes. Go.

I can remember like it was yesterday, although it was ten years ago. My little boy, Alex, was just five years old. It was at Ritenour Junior High. He was just about to come out of the locker room. My wife, Monique, and I were waiting, and he walked out for the first time ever with his basketball uniform on, and the expression was priceless—so proud, so happy. For my wife, it was no big deal. I don't cry at movies, but I broke down. I saw myself at the exact same age. I saw me in that jersey. My wife saw the tears coming down and promptly said, "Man up."

—Frank Cusumano, KSDK sports

Chapter Six

Months **18-24**: Too Early to Teach Them to Make a Martini?

By now it's likely hit you (as reality sometimes does): Wow, I guess it'll be *years* before I can make him mow the lawn. Yes, that's true. Being a dad allows you to conjure up "to do" lists and "chores for which I'll pay you a quarter," but now you're realizing that in addition to being too short, the would-be manservant probably isn't ready to clean your gutters.

And, alas, it's too soon to have him make a reliable martini. According to Dr. Edgar Greygoose at Washington University's Research Center for Particularly Useful Children (RCPUC), "While some especially gifted children have been trained in such a manner, our extensive studies show the toddler routinely chooses again and again to use way too much vermouth. Also, two out of five have been found to poke their eye with the toothpick."

The good news is Dr. Greygoose and his team are working on genetically altering embryos to allow toddlers to make you a fine drink. So wish him well, and maybe that miracle of science will be ready in time for your second child!

Meanwhile, if you're outside, and the cooler is only a few feet away, you might be able to train the child to get you a Bud Light. Ahh, the joys of fatherhood!

UNDERSTANDING "NO," "DANGER," AND "YUCKY"

It's time the kid understands "no," and thus, you must lay down boundaries. Being firm and consistent is key. With "firm" we're looking for a sharp, solid, but non-screaming vocalized *"no,"* usually accompanied by a careful yet authoritative grip on the kid pulling him away from whatever may have his interest at the moment. This will almost always make him cry, but don't give in—he really shouldn't be chewing on your collection of Cardinals baseball cards from the 1970s, no matter how cute he looks doing it.

You're a simple guy, so you'll appreciate another simple word: "danger." In the same tone of voice as "no," use "danger" when the kid is near stairs, trying to climb on something he could fall off of, or starting to read your wife's *O* magazine. Being consistent with this will teach him that when he hears that word, he needs to back away before he gets seriously hurt.

So when you're preparing for the guys to come over to watch the game, and you have the crock-pot brewing with some serious hot wing action, and you spot your little girl starting to pull on the cord, "danger" is much better than "Don't do that or you'll pull all the scalding hot wings down on your head, and we'll be left to snack on stale pretzels!"

Rounding out your Assortment of Assertions is the beloved word "yucky." This one doesn't need to be said with quite the vocal force of the other two, but having the child learn the word will come in handy when he does things like try to dump the kitty litter on his head, crawl into the toilet bowl, or run for city alderman.

Learning those three words followed by removal from the scene will be effective in training the toddling toddler. As for him tearing up the latest issue of *O* you can just say you didn't see him do it.

Earnin' Their Keep

You can and should prepare your child for the day she hedges the bushes and builds you a new patio deck before she goes to her Brownie meeting by establishing a "habit of helping." As soon as she can understand, include her in helping out with "chores." Now, the reality is it'll be more trouble to have her "help" than for you to just do it yourself, but it's important to give her the chance to participate. Plus, it will make her feel valuable, which, of course, she is.

One good task is helping pick up her toys. Made-on-the-spot clean-up songs help it go better, and an established routine of picking up the toys at the end of the day is definitely something you're going to want to establish. You could also have her help feed the dog—even if this involves you handing her the cup of food and letting her walk it over to the dish (and at best, achieving only a 40 percent accuracy rate when dumping the food in the dish).

As she grows older, continue upping the responsibility. But don't get lazy and just take care of everything yourself—it sets a bad precedent, and she'll just grow up never wanting to work and getting a job at the DMV.

THOSE KIDS—THEY'RE PORTABLE!

Typically, you'll be slaving away from 9 to 5 on weekdays, spending the precious few evening hours with your beautiful baby. The weekend will come, and there'll be opportunities to take them to the park or the zoo. Sometimes Mom will need a break, so you might even get to spend some one-on-one time doing something fun.

But alas, life will get in the way. There will be plenty of Saturdays when you just have to run errands. Oil changes, hardware store runs, and trips to Bass Pro Shop for that upcoming trip to the Ozarks are a necessity. The first instinct is to just leave the kid at home. It would be much faster to just do this on your own, and how much fun would hanging out in the plumbing aisle at Lowe's be to a toddler, anyway?

The great news is it's very fun for kids to run around with their dads, especially if you put in a little bit of effort. Everything is new to a kid, and especially since he doesn't get to spend as much time with you as either of you want, this is a great opportunity for bonding. When you're at the stores, constantly talk about what you're seeing—"Ooooo! Look at the riding mowers! Want to crawl on them?" (Go ahead and let him as long as no one is looking.) Also, if you're standing there discussing which toilet handle will hold up the best, ask his opinion! He'll likely have one. (Hint: He'll go for the one that tastes the best.)

The Importance of Reading

There is going to be a natural tendency to divvy up certain duties between Mom and Dad, but reading is one task that is extremely important to share. Dads need to do this, especially with their sons. Boys who grow up with only Mom reading to them get the message that reading is just a "girl" thing, so it's critical to let boys crawl up on your lap and read.

And even if you have a girl, it's still another important source of bonding.

Likely they will get stuck on certain books, and you'll have to read them over and over again until you really "goodnight" that moon in a way Tony Soprano would. But you have to remember that you're reading for them, not you.

Fun Fact!

Kids don't know the difference between new and used, and the stuff's just going to get broken anyway, so your salvation will be the garage sales that you never noticed before, but now you see everywhere. Man, are these a deal. You can always find cars and dolls and even those cute little kitchens that Toys "R" Us sells for like $200 for pennies on the dollar. Go to the fancier neighborhoods!

Should you be able to coax them into letting you choose, here are some especially dad-friendly books: *What Dads Can't Do* by Douglas Wood; *My Dad* by Anthony Brown; *Chugga Chugga Choo Choo* by Kevin Lewis; anything by Mercer Mayer; and anything by Byron Barton.

MUSIC, PART II

Now it's time to start exposing the kids to some of that wonderful St. Louis music. Anything in Chuck Berry's catalog is good, but you'll find your baby swaying best to his *The Definitive Collection: Chuck Berry* (and its great complement, *You Came a Long Way from St. Louis: The Many Sides of Chuck Berry*). It'll likely inspire you to go catch Chuck some Wednesday in the Duck Room—leaving the kid at home, of course.

Not quite on the level of Chuck, but producing CDs that are enjoyable to all toddlers, and the toddler in all of us, is local kids' entertainer Babaloo (www.babaloomusicandfun.com). Definitely try to catch his act—it's high energy and will distract your kids for more than a while.

You can't expose them too soon to these two musical geniuses, and let us tell you, they beat the hell out of listening to Raffi!

SHE SHOOTS, SHE SCORES!

With an eye on your daughter eventually getting one of those big, gaudy World Series rings, you can now lay the foundation of those athletic skills that you yourself were born with, but alas, were denied being fully developed by that jerk Coach Mac who would never, EVER, seriously consider you for halfback, and thus, you've been forced to live your life as a lie, and now you live out your life doing whatever job you do, a pale shadow of what your potential sports ability could have reached had you just had a *little* encouragement, a *little* opportunity instead of being squished like a junebug by that egghead of a coach.

But we digress—this is about the kid.

So we've done the knocking-down-blocks thing, now we need to work more on stacking. It's a crucial time for her, so spend some time on the floor working with the blocks—the goal is to stack at least three or four of them. Demonstrate what to do and show an unusual amount of enthusiasm when she does it. You know, pretend Jeff Wilkins just kicked the winning field goal.

Also, keep lots of balls around. Probably not regulation NFL footballs or NBA basketballs but look for the soft, smaller, rubbery ones. We're looking for her to throw it BAMN-style (By Any Means Necessary), and she should be able to kick it as well.

While kicking and throwing a ball is to be expected and encouraged at this stage, if she's able to launch a bruising, nose-breaking full body check against a Detroit Red Wings hockey player, especially if it's early in the season, it's likely a problem. You should probably get her to a social worker, or an excellent sports agent, depending on your disposition.

Also in the gross motor department (no, this doesn't include what she can do with strained peas), she should be able to trot at this point, even if it's stiffly. This will drive Mom to serious nail biting, but you, being a guy, will be cool with the running and the inevitable falling down. I mean, it's part of life. Hell, *you* still fall down. And when she does, rather than over-reacting and picking her up right away and thus freaking her out, just show a little empathy.

WORDS TO LIVE BY

Okay! Not that you're keeping score, but we're looking for her to be saying twenty to fifty words. No, "Na na na na, na na na na, hey hey, good-bye" does NOT count as twelve. That only counts as . . . well, it doesn't really count at all.

Fun Fact!

While it's too early to officially start toilet training in a hardcore manner, the groundwork needs to be laid at this point. You need to be observant and learn to tell when she's sitting there pooping. Learn the facial mannerism that accompanies this act, then seize the opportunity, labeling it: "Are you pooping? You're pooping, aren't you?" Now, it's harder for the dad because you're likely not around the kid as much as Mom. Don't fret—practice on your co-workers. Learn to recognize that slightly quizzical look, then go, "I don't mean to interrupt your Powerpoint presentation on our past marketing efforts, but Jill, are you pooping? You look like you're pooping."

Again, we have the "Dada" thing. "Dog" is another good one. "Car" is a good one. "Mama" should be coming into play here. Anything close to the seven dirty words you can't say on television means you are doing a very bad job at controlling your "colorful" vocabulary.

Look for him to, and encourage him to, parrot what you are saying. Continue to label household objects . . . the ones the *kid* is interested in. That would be of the spoon/stuffed animal/Lego variety. He won't be that interested in your new lawn mower, but what the heck, talk to him about it anyway. You never know.

BABYSITTERS

Around this time the novelty and thrill of your ability to procreate is likely waning on your immediate family. It's easy to trust your parents, her parents, and those siblings with a relatively short criminal record with watching your precious toddler while you scoot out to dinner or, God forbid, even get to see one of those "movie" things.

But they will start to realize, "Hey, we have lives too!" and will not always be available. Also, you might realize that they tend to just put on a video and drink your beer. Maybe a *paid* sitter would play and interact with the kid? And maybe, just maybe, that would be a better thing?

Hopefully your neighbors with kids will have some suggestions. But this will likely be another source of conflict between you and the missus, especially if you have to pursue someone cold. Typically, a neighbor will know of some young girl who likes to play with kids and is always hungry for money to spend at the Chesterfield Mall. If you're already enrolled in a Gymboree or Little Gym kind of place, there are almost always notices up there, and they are probably the best place to start.

But your standards for whom to leave the kid with might be somewhat different than your wife's.

You'll be focused on the idea of just getting out of the house, so someone with "666" tattooed on her face might seem fine to you. She's going to be looking for someone more toward the raised-by-the-Contemplative-Nuns-of-Belleville end of the spectrum.

You will eventually find someone, and it's always best to do a short trial run: Just two hours in the early evening, getting back before dark, and making sure that it seems to have gone well before you move on to longer stretches. Your wife will want to call her every five minutes, but do your best to keep it to just one or two calls per hour. Eventually, you'll get a good or not-so-good vibe on how it goes. But thinking long-term, you'll want to start a business relationship with some girl who is going to engage the kid, someone who is going to be fun as opposed to throwing him in the playpen and spending the entire time text-messaging some guy in Wentzville.

Age-wise, it has to be a pretty exceptional twelve year old, and once they start getting over sixteen, you end up having to pay significantly more (then again, they can usually drive themselves, which is a pretty nifty advantage, often worth the extra bucks). But somewhere in that range is good. Pay is typically five to seven dollars an hour for someone under fifteen, with a small tip—you know, rounding up.

If you really want to retain a good sitter, you will end up becoming a slave to the clock. In other words, come home when you say you will, if you want to keep her happy. No saying you'll be home by 11:00, but then when having so much fun at Harrah's, you don't get home until 1:00. Not only is this rude and irresponsible, it will annoy her parents.

And along these lines, a quality babysitter will likely have many suitors, so it's up to you to gain the competitive edge. This can be gained by making sure your house is stacked with such babysitter-friendly accoutrements as Fritos, popcorn, Pringles, Ding Dongs, Oreos, quality frozen pizza, and a generous selection of soda—and make sure she knows where to find them. Be sure she knows how to work all

---

DIDIA KNOW?

January 2 is not too soon to hire a babysitter for the next New Year's Eve!

---

the remotes, and tell her she's free to use the phone and/or Internet. These things, tipping generously, and telling her how much your kid loves her, will all go a long way toward ensuring she'll always want to babysit for you *first* (unlike the Nelsons down the street who only leave out granola and don't even have cable, leaving her to watch reruns of *The Lawrence Welk Show*).

WHERE TO TAKE AN 18-24 MONTH OLD

Things are getting better! Generally. Restaurants are still dicey but are more do-able. She is starting to really appreciate the zoo and story time, and if you've done your job, she is beginning to interact with other kids her age. If you're lucky enough to have friends with a kid of similar age, there is nothing better than having picnics or the preferred combination happy hour/play date.

OH MY GOSH—I HAVE THE KID FOR THE DAY!

In good weather, one of the nicest things you can do is head south to Suson Park in South County. This small gem of a park has a great little "farm" complete with horse stables. Two small lakes that are appropriate for toddling around make it an especially good place to spend a morning (before it gets too hot). Otherwise, in bad weather, there are always the Westfield malls with playgrounds. If you're feeling more adventurous, take the MetroLink to the downtown library. The travelin' is more than half the fun. If they don't have a special exhibit, they have a great selection of children's books, so sit down, plop her on your lap, and go through a few!

CHAPTER SIX
REVIEW QUESTIONS

1. Match the action by your child on the left with the proper response on the right:

1) Puts dog food in mouth a) "No"

2) Heads toward basement stairwell b) "Good"

3) Starts to pick up your water cup from c) "Yucky"
   coffee table

4) Pays just $225 over wholesale price d) "Danger"
   for a brand new Saturn Relay from
   Lou Fusz St. Charles

2. Which of these errands is *not* appropriate to take your kid along on?

      A. Golf Headquarters

      B. Lowe's Hardware

      C. Border's Books

      D. Beer tasting at Fast Eddie's

3. What's the greatest thing about Chuck Berry?

      A. He's true to his St. Louis roots

      B. He's the real king of rock and roll

      C. His music is great at any age

      D. He didn't write "Shake My Sillies Out"

4. What is the most important quality you look for in a babysitter?

      A. She's taken a babysitting class

      B. She genuinely loves to play with kids

      C. She only has five face piercings

      D. She's breathing

5. Short Essay: Compare and contrast the benefits of having your child help by picking up her toys vs. building a new patio deck with a Jacuzzi.

When Timmy was in first grade, he came home with a note from the teacher. She wanted to make an appointment to discuss his behavior. So I made the appointment, went to meet with her, and she told me that he would have to clean up his act or they'd have to send him back to kindergarten. So I went home that night, and Timmy and I had our first father-son talk. I told him what the teacher said, and he looked at me and said, "I don't have to behave." I said, "Excuse me?" He said, "No, I don't have to go to school, because when I grow up I'm going to play baseball for the St. Louis Cardinals."

—Timothy J. McKernan about son, St. Louis sportscaster Tim McKernan

Chapter Seven

Terrible Twos, and Why a Do-It-Yourself Home Vasectomy Is Looking Pretty Good

Here's the dirty little secret they don't tell you about the infamous "Terrible Twos": They usually kick in around eighteen months! Of course, we're not helping by telling you this *now*—as it's information you needed about seven pages ago—but it doesn't really matter since nothing can prepare you for it anyway. It's sort of like being run over by a Metro St. Louis Sewer truck.

The most important thing for a St. Louis Dad to remember during this time is the simplest: YOU'RE THE DAD. Remain calm at all times when faced with tantrums and behavior one normally associates with ne'er-do-wells at Soulard Mardi Gras. Your little monster *wants* to get to you, wants to see you get unraveled—don't give him the satisfaction.

When meltdowns, screaming fits, etc., happen, you need to step up and put on your game face. Be strong, be firm; don't even THINK of raising your voice, let alone a hand—it's a sign of weakness. You lived through the seven years we didn't have professional football here, so you can handle this.

Good Cop/Bad Cop

Many clichés are based in reality, and the idea that one parent can play the part of the good cop and the other play the Harvey Keitel role usually comes to fruition, and usually (but not exclusively) this falls along gender lines.

This can come in very handy, and we urge you to exploit the possibilities to your full advantage.

During this time the child finds it extremely difficult to cooperate in the smallest of tasks— getting dressed, picking up toys, doing the laundry without adding too much starch, etc. Usually Mom is involved in supervising those chores and will be at her wit's end. She is the source of comfort and

Didja Know?

Kids will be testing you all the time. Be sure to always have a number two pencil ready, make sure you fill in the oval completely, and keep your eyes on your own paper.

the source of food, and the kid will manipulate that and exploit it to his advantage. The professionals call this "testing your limits," whereas you'll prefer a more earthy term for it, something commonly heard in locker rooms.

THE "PICKY" EATER

This is another in a series of things that will drive your wife crazy, and you'll have to be the voice of reason.

Definitely give it the ol' college try, but the kid is going to eat what the kid is going to eat. You'll rationalize with your wife, saying that *all* your friends are having problems getting their kids to eat anything beyond crackers, chicken fingers, and the stuff on the floor that may or may not be toxic. But while you might have had success prior to this stage with getting the kid to eat a corn kernel or even some pieces of apples fresh from the Soulard

Farmer's Market, he'll likely start to only eat cheerios, French fries, crackers, and the little rocks in your backyard.

Here's something to keep in mind: His appetite is decreasing at this point, so you have less leverage. Now, the Mom-type person may inadvertently make mealtime a "battle." This is not the way to go on too many levels to list—but first and foremost, it makes it difficult for you to enjoy *your* Imo's Bacon/Sausage/Canadian Bacon/Oh Yeah Still More Bacon pizza.

That said:

- Always try to eat as a family. Establish the routine and basically keep it as long as you can. No TV during dinner. Get the kid used to what it's all about: Family-time conversation.
- Make sure the kid isn't over-juiced. Keep juice to a minimum and water it down: No more than four ounces a day (i.e., a third of what would fit in a can of beer, assuming it's not tallboy night).
- Constantly offer food to the kid, but be cool about it. Put a little piece of pizza or green bean or whatever you're eating on his plate. Let him discover the certain, how you say, *je ne sais quoi* of the toasted ravioli or throw it in the dog's dish. Sure, likely it'll be the latter, but *whatever* his choice, be cool about it.

We strongly recommend there be no battling over food. Life is too short. When he's fifteen, you can take him out to the Eternity Vegetarian Deli & Juice Bar on Euclid and tell him to eat his sprouts or you won't let him get his driver's license until he's forty-three. But until then . . .

Watch What You Talk About

About this time, you may realize that your kid is listening to and noticing things around him. Specifically, everything you do and say. You'll start to realize, often with great horror, that you've given birth to a combination surveillance camera–cartoon parrot (you know, the kind that immediately repeats whole sentences). But while he doesn't live on the bottom of the sea, or reside next to the sink, believe us: The seed of your loins has turned into a little sponge.

And this sponge doesn't turn off, so it's great when you're espousing your well-conceived theories about how we can overcome state budget deficits without raising taxes, but not so great when you're spouting off on your brother's totally annoying girlfriend and comparing her clothes to something a lady of ill repute might wear, and then you wonder aloud how he could date someone who is such a . . . something that rhymes with "pitch." Your boy will start to see his favorite uncle in an entirely new light—you know, one as stark and unflattering as what's in the bathroom at the downtown Greyhound Bus Station on 13th Street.

Typically, while driving home from a family event, you might want to go off on Uncle Ernie for being a big loud drunk who can't pay his bills and Cousin Edna, who's looser than a Casino Queen penny slot machine, but show some restraint. Don't let your son pick up your not-so-subtle negative vibes and cross words—because he won't be able to figure out that you love Uncle Ernie to death and Cousin Edna is your favorite family member and you are just blowing off steam.

Save it for when he is put to bed and out of earshot.

This also goes for the extra *fun* future plans that may or may not end up happening. For example, if you think you can casually say on a Wednesday, "I'm thinking of taking him to the Magic House, then to McDonald's, the one on Kirkwood Road with the big play area, this Saturday, and then to Ted Drewes for the largest concrete ever" and have him *not* go absolutely crazy, and thus drive you crazy for days, well . . . let's just say it's a mistake you make *once*.

Providing your bright, yet not-sure-of-how-the-space/time-continuum-works spawn with information about play dates, visits with especially fun family members, or a trip to Target where he can look at the Thomas the Train toys any more than four minutes before you walk out the door is likely to cause great grief and agony.

And God help you if you say something like, "We're going to Grant's Farm with your favorite playmate Cora this Saturday!" on a Wednesday. Even if you live through him asking if it's Saturday yet every five minutes, undoubtedly, come Saturday there'll be a torrential downpour with Kent Ehrhardt saying he's sure a tornado that registers an F4 on the Fujita-Pearson Scale will come up north on I-270, get off at Gravois, and head toward the Steak 'n Shake by River des Peres causing a path of certain death and destruction. Suddenly, Grant's Farm is not such a good idea, and when you have to explain that to your kid . . . well, it'll be a long, ugly afternoon all the way around.

BE SILLY

It's not the kind of thing you would want your Mizzou fraternity brothers to see, but it's important that you bring yourself down to the kid's level. And let's admit it—for most of us, it's not really that far to go.

Silly rhymes, silly walks, silly faces, silly talk—all count toward play. Making up nonsensical games

FUN FACT!

You thought your days of spelling bees were long gone, but boy oh boy are they back! You will need to hone your ability to not only spell things on the fly ("Your sister is such an i-d-i-o-t"), but alas, you'll have to decipher things your wife is saying to you. She'll be like, "I talked to the rabbi today, and he confirmed the date for the c-i-r-c-u-m-c-i-s-i-o-n," and you'll be left standing in silence wondering why the rabbi cares what day he goes to the circus mission, or even what a circus mission is.

is another winner. Pretend the cat is talking to you. Have the spoon and the fork suddenly break into a demonstration of martial arts, complete with its own soundtrack (we suggest "Kung Fu Fighting" or the closing-credit orchestrated score to *Crouching Tiger, Hidden Dragon*). Pretend to eat one of her toys, have it "go down your throat" into your shirt, suddenly look like you're queasy, and then "throw it up." (This also kills at most corporate Christmas parties—just replace "toy" with "stapler" and wait for further hijinks to ensue!)

Lead by example in coming up with imaginative ways to play, and for God's sake, don't let your wife videotape you doing it.

Choose Your Battles

Kids are going to want to explore and try everything, and it's going to be tempting to say, "No, don't do that" to everything she does that is remotely odd—because, well, everything she does is very odd. Before you start to move and pull her away, quickly ask yourself what harm is being done.

It becomes the time of "relativity" and we don't mean Einstein's theory (the scientist, not the guy the bagel store is named after). This is not

$$E = MC^2,$$

It's more like

$$C + PC \times TV^{TTB} / \infty = BFD$$

That is: "Chewing on Plastic Coasters, then going over to the Television, and Throwing Them Behind the TV, and doing this forever or until he's done this to all twenty-four coasters, is, in the big scheme of things, not a big frickin' deal."

After all, you've just stopped and yelled at her for trying to ram a metal fork into a light socket, yanking your pit bull's tail, and spraying bug spray into her mouth—all in the previous three minutes. So if she is "playing" with the coasters . . . no big deal, right?

THE TIME OUT

Tantrums are going to happen. You will think they are designed specifically to get your goat, and you're not too far off. So what you need to be aware of is that should she *succeed* in getting you all riled up, then the little thing "wins." Rumor has it that you're the adult, so the more calm you can remain during a meltdown, the better off you'll be.

Sometimes you can reason with her, as in, "Are you mad because I won't let you eat this entire box of Little Debbie snack cakes?" but usually it's just already spun way out of control, and you have no choice but to resort to the "time out."

The time out is when you make the kid sit down for a set time (usually anything from two to ten minutes). Where this time out happens is very important, as it might send mixed messages. For example, you don't want to do it in her bed/crib, because then she'll start to associate her bed with punishment. Same with the playpen. Ditto for the Page Extension.

You'll come to enjoy the power of the "Time Out." Unfortunately, local scientists have been unable to transfer it to the outside world. So if you get a home assessment from the county that is clearly way off base in what your house is worth, while you can *call* Charlie Dooley's office and threaten the county executive a "time out" if your taxes go up because of a bone-headed assessor, it probably won't work. That said, it has been known to work on mayors in places like Overland.

Most Dads find a corner away from play toys most effective for this. When you get really mad you might be tempted to do something harsher, like making her watch HGTV. This is not recommended, if for any other reason than if you start being that brutal this early on, what can you build to? Save it for when she's fourteen and has burned down the garage or something.

RATIONALIZATION

Sometimes you'll be tempted to apply your God-given logical view of the world to a misbehaving tot. Save it for the Charlack cop who pulls you over on I-170 for doing 62 in a 60 zone (and it'll have pretty much the same impact—which is to say, none). Pretty much consider your kid's inability to accept the "if you do *x*, you can't do *y*" at this stage. For example, if he is misbehaving and it's close to the time of the day you let him watch a thirty-minute video (as in, say, ten minutes close) you *might* have success with, "If you don't stop smashing all of Mommy's Vienna-made ceramic unicorns against the head of your Uncle Julio there, you can't watch *Teletubbies*." But if you go any further out, they can't comprehend time and consequences.

So, "If you don't stop that right now, you can't go to Amanda's birthday party at Gymboree tomorrow" is completely lost on a kid this age. So is "If you don't stop that right now, you can't go to Grant's Farm when it opens in the spring, approximately four and a half months away, not counting daylight savings time."

For really serious infractions, you might try, "If you don't step away from my Bob Gibson bobble-head, I'll make you go to college at Rolla and major in computer science," but don't plan on success there.

On another note: Be wary of any punishment that actually punishes *you*. Not letting them watch their video means, well—that's thirty minutes you were going to spend raking the leaves or cutting the grass. Do the math on whatever approach you take.

Public Meltdowns

It's one thing to contain a temper-tantrum-prone kid in the house, but when you're out in public, all bets are off. Women tend to get more embarrassed when the kid starts screaming, "I hate you, I hate you" and pulling on the clothes rack at the Ann Taylor store at Plaza Frontenac. Luckily, growing up in St. Louis with the type of guys you hang out with, your embarrassment bar is much higher. You've carried your cousin Rudy out of McGurk's in Soulard after he actually tried the "If I told you you had a beautiful body would you hold it against me?" line on the waitress.

Being a Dad allows you to take swift action. When you see her going over the edge, give her the ol' "I'm going to count to three," and at two and a half, if there's no chance of her calming down, grab her and march her out of the store. Yes, she might still be screaming, and you might be getting looks (though trust us—the vast majority will be sympathetic). Then once in the car, go directly home in complete silence. Don't yell, don't discuss—being the strong, silent type is most effective.

Under no circumstance should you bribe. No "If you stop kicking the store clerk and pulling on her hair, Daddy will take you to Crown Candy for the biggest ice cream sundae ever!" Your instincts will tell you to not negotiate with the little terrorist, and you should listen to your instincts on this one.

So maybe you won't be able to buy the motor oil you needed for the lawn mower, but this is just the cost of doing business. If you always wanted to keep your lawn mower properly functioning . . . well, you should have thought of that before you went and started a family.

WHERE TO TAKE A TWO-YEAR-OLD

The closer they get to three, the more in the clear you are, in general. If you can keep to their naptime schedule, and always keep crackers and raisins in the backpack, there's not much you can't do. Stay away from some of the louder, more crowded festivals, parades, and street parties. And taking them to movies at this age is dicey, as there is little that can hold their attention and/or not scare them. It's too early for the major sports events, but it's a great time to start hitting those church and school carnivals that pop up.

Oh My Gosh—I Have the Kid for the Day!

At one point it was dirty and not much to look at, but boy, have they cleaned up and improved upon the Museum of Transportation. If your kid is into anything with wheels (and what two-year-old isn't?), this is a great place to go. In addition to being able to climb on the trains, take a little ride, and look in the airplanes and boats, you can play in a special room of cool toys called Creation Station (it costs extra—$1.50 per person—but it's worth it). Bring a magazine or your paper and sit and watch him or her go to town!

CHAPTER SEVEN
REVIEW QUESTIONS

1. True or False: A do-it-yourself home vasectomy is the best damn idea you ever had.

2. If you're going to be the "bad cop" to your wife's good cop, who is *not* a good role model?

    A. Vic Mackey

    B. John McTiernan

    C. Jimmy "Popeye" Doyle

    D. Barney Fife

3. If you're "choosing your battles," which of the following can you "let go" of?

    A. Pulling pots and pans out of a kitchen cabinet

    B. Licking your DVD of *Goodfellas*

    C. Tearing your latest copy of *Maxim* to shreds

    D. Waterloo

4. Which of the following is *not* an appropriate place to have a "time out"?

    A. Playpen

    B. Kitchen corner

    C. Blues penalty box, especially when Jamal Mayers is already there

    D. The Hooters on Lackland

5. Short Essay: 500 words on the following topic: "Bribing a two-and-a-half-year-old to behave well in a public place is like giving tax breaks to build a new casino in South County because . . ."

I took my son Ben to Crestwood Park for his first downhill sledding adventure when he was three. With Ben sitting in front of me on the plastic toboggan, my weight and the steep hill produced a faster ride than expected, and when we finally stopped he was crying because it looked like someone painfully shot a big snowcone at his face. But when I asked if he wanted to go again, the tears stopped, and through a broad grin he screamed, "Yeah!"

—Dan Martin, *St. Louis Post-Dispatch* cartoonist

CHAPTER EIGHT

THEY ARE THREE! AND WHY THE WIGGLES ARE A THREAT TO OUR NATIONAL SANITY

Moms will insist that the baby's personality starts showing on about day six. ("Look at the way he spit up all over your new bowling shirt—he has such personality!") But to Dad, the thing you spawned starts becoming a person around this age. Likes and dislikes become more pronounced—on some occasions, a little too pronounced.

Sadly, you'll wake up at some point during this period and find your house overrun with videos and CDs that were created by clearly demented individuals. At the top of your child's list of questionable preferences will likely be the Wiggles. This quartet of geeks from Down Under are a force to be reckoned with. What's most off-putting is not that they don't have any talent, can't write songs, can't play instruments, can't sing, and probably have never been kissed by a girl—it's that they are all that AND they have more money than God and Augie Busch combined.

When exposed to the Wiggles, you'll likely come to the same conclusion that a local organization has. Our own respected Ballwin Academy of Detrimental Melodies Utilized Scandalously against Innocent Children (B.A.D.M.U.S.I.C.) released a study in 2006 that concluded that the Wiggles have many similarities to the communists of yesteryear:

- Both are an affront to free societies;
- Both have singing skills that would get them kicked out of Tom's Bar & Grill on karaoke night;
- Both are mysteriously well financed (though one was financed by Marxists, the other begrudgingly by beaten-down parents);
- Both usually appear in black boots.

For the sake of our nation's sanity, when they first emerged in the early 1990s President George H. W. Bush should have led the country to fighting the Wiggles in Australia before they followed us home. Now they are on our shores, DVD players, and children's pillowcases. Oh, the humanity!

It is much healthier to introduce little Albert to the cool sounds of Miles Davis. *Kind of Blue* is a great album to listen to while they are stacking up and knocking down blocks, for example. And what could be better than Erin Bode's *Don't Take Your Time* for playing catch with a beach ball? These are just two great examples—of local artists no doubt—that are much better for the soul and the intellect than the Wiggles' "Romp Bomp a Stomp."

Jazz is great for stimulating little minds, and our Gateway City has an embarrassment of riches in the blues and jazz genres. As far as we're concerned, you can't expose your kids too early to this great music. So if you don't already have the CDs of Clark Terry, Kim Massie, Johnnie Johnson, Billy Peek, Scott Joplin, and many other past and present musicians with St. Louis roots, by all means, pick some up.

POTTY TRAINING

Like a typical guy, anything to do with the dreaded "potty" portion of the child-rearing is something you've likely avoided. You've probably let your wife

Fun Fact!

Did you know "Barney" is Latin for "Satan"? It's true . . . look it up.

handle this task, while you took care of the more "manly" aspects of fatherhood, such as taking little Claire to Chesterfield Billiards and teaching her the importance of a nice bank shot.

If you're lucky, your wife has successfully potty trained the kid by now, and man, are you off the hook. If not, it's time to get involved and help out (and we mean more than just plopping the kid down and letting her watch some video with a title like *Big Blue Bear in the Big Beige Bathroom Takes a Grand Gigantic Poop*.)

If little or no progress has been made, it's time to double-team the kid. There is no one secret method that works on all kids, and you'll find yourself obsessively discussing this matter with your friends. Extremes include letting the kid wander around your backyard naked from the waist down in the hopes that soiling her own body will make her think, "Hey! Maybe I should learn to do something about this." Some swear by this, but most have not been successful.

Kids are crazy about stickers, so arrange a chart of twenty or twenty-five squares, and reward them with one every time they make it to the bathroom in time. When they fill up the chart, they get a present. Slightly more controversial is switching out stickers for candy, like M&Ms—"controversial" in that you'll hear a lot of experts warn against bribing with food; however, the reality is M&Ms top a Care Bear sticker any day.

Make a big production of buying her big girl underwear at the store. Make her feel like it's a rite of passage, and make sure she does things like call Grandma and tell her about it when you get home from the store.

Letting her wear the new underwear (around the house only) works because unlike those diapers, if she soils herself she is incredibly uncomfortable, and that tends to hammer the message home. Once she starts making it to the bathroom in time, heap lots of praise on her. Inevitably, she will have a few "accidents" after that; always treat them as such, as opposed to getting mad at her.

Fun Fact!

Kids get to wear fun underwear! They make them with Dora the Explorer, Clifford the Big Red Dog, and even Spider Man and Batman. But before you get excited and ask the clerk at Target for something like that in your size, know that they are only for kids.

Playing Well with Others

It's a critical time in the socialization of your little girl, and Dad's firm hand and leadership skills should be a guiding force as she learns how to play, interact, and simply "be" with other kids. Typically at the playground, family events, play dates, and monster truck rallies, Mom will quickly jump up at the sign of a snotty nose or a slightly askew hair. Your attention needs to focus on how your child plays with other kids.

We recommend zero tolerance for inappropriate behavior like pushing, not sharing, and temper tantrums. Being so vigilant can sometimes be tedious, but it will pay off in the short run *and* the long run—through their teens and beyond. If you choose to laugh off bad behavior, you do it at your own peril. (Sure, those guys on *Jackass* may be millionaires, but do you really want to spend your Christmas Eves with Johnny Knoxville, Jr.?)

So when she runs up to little cousin Luke, who is only two, takes his truck, and pushes him down, and Luke just explodes in tears, the Three Stooges fan in you will likely want to laugh, because let's be honest: It's kinda funny. But the dad in you needs to be on your feet and in motion faster than if the bartender at Blueberry Hill had just shouted "Free Amberbock!"

Take her firmly, look her in the eye, and explain in short, terse terms that she is displaying unacceptable behavior. "Luke is only two, and he is our guest, so just find something else to play with. That is how we act in this house. Do you understand?"

Don't raise your voice. It's less effective than calm, measured tones. And repeat this as often as necessary.

One of the tools in your arsenal is her desire for your approval. Use it wisely in shaping her socialization skills. Likewise, keep your eyes out for especially good behavior. When she's playing with said truck and little Luke comes over and takes it from her, and she shrugs it off and plays with something else, make a note to comment on it later. At bedtime, tell her, "I was very proud of you today when Luke took that toy from you and you let him. He's younger than you and doesn't know better, and with his loser of a dad, my lame-ass brother-in-law who can't seem to hold a decent job and barely knows how to dress himself, he might not ever figure it out . . . but you were a very good girl and Daddy is very proud of you."

That approach will go far.

Although maybe you shouldn't say the "lame-ass brother-in-law" part.

BE A "WHY NOT?" DAD

On the plus side, kids are blossoming into wonderfully weird beings now. What amuses them, what fascinates them, is as unpredictable as it is unusual. You'll have a knee-jerk reaction of saying, "Don't do that!" to odd behavior like taking the cushions on and off the couch or taking pots and pans out of the kitchen cabinets and banging on them with one of your remotes.

Sure, there is plenty of behavior that is inappropriate. But a lot of kids' behavior is just their way of exploring the world. The challenge is to understand that you're going to have to say "no" to a lot of things (like the staple gun), so try to let as much as possible go (for example, that remote she is using on the pans—it's for the VCR, which you rarely use anymore, anyway).

So before you admonish them for some behavior, ask yourself, "Why not?" If they are getting their kicks playing with the sofa cushions, running back and forth between the front door and the TV making curiously odd guttural noises, or saying inappropriate things about your mother-in-law that they may or may not have heard from you, if there's no chance of someone getting hurt and little chance of something *really* important getting broken, let it go. Let them be kids.

Didja Know?

The Humanitarian Institute of Social Scientists Understanding Children and Kids Society (T.H.I.S.S.U.C.K.S.) recently released a report from its Hillsboro-based trailer park that says more men lose more of their hair when they are raising a two-year-old than at any other time in their life.

GAMES

Kids this age want to play games, but they don't really get it. Still, as Dad, you must enforce the rules of *Candyland*. Mom will often smile and look the other way when little Claire picks the Mr. Mint card, but instead of moving her piece back there, moves it all the way up to Queen Frostine.

Not you. You will rightly have the urge to teach her at an early age that cheating is wrong and doesn't get you ahead in life (save for politicians, an increasing number of professional athletes, and cell phone companies). You make her go all the way back to the beginning of the board, even if it means another ten minutes of playing the irritating game. While you might be tempted to just think, well what can it hurt if I pretend to look away while the kid digs through the stack of cards looking for the one that will ultimately move the game along faster . . . and that day, it won't really matter. But if she gets in the habit of deceiving, she'll likely be no fun to play with when she's nine, and an attorney for a utility company when she's an adult.

The rules are simple:

- Don't cheat—not even as a joke.
- Don't let her cheat *ever*.
- Don't let her win . . . at least not by too much or too often.
- Don't beat her mercilessly and then boast about it. Beating the crap out of your kid playing Cariboo is much less impressive than beating your college buddy at foosball.

FUN FACT!

From around now until he is like twelve, fourteen, or twenty-seven, depending on how bright he is, you can get him to do almost *anything* by "timing" him. Like say, "Let's pick up all your toy cars . . . I'll time ya! Go! 1 . . . 2 . . . 3. . . ." Or even "Go get daddy the bag of Doritos . . . I'll time ya! Go! 1 . . . 2 . . . 3. . . ." Before he can think about it, he's off and running. Works like a charm.

Since the first time human beings formed social groups, games have been used to teach children cooperation and respect. Today that even applies to *Chutes and Ladders.*

LAME GAMES TO PLAY WHEN YOU DON'T FEEL LIKE MOVING

Nothing is more fun than making up a game, especially if it's a game that involves you either lying on your back on the floor or sitting on the couch having a cold one. So these two are great ones—you can make up your own titles, but for now let's call them . . .

The Airplane Game

Sit on the couch. Have a beer. Have your kid sit next to you. Pretend you're flying an airplane. "Where do you want to go today?" And then discuss the possibilities if she doesn't come up with something immediately. "It's cold here, would you like to go to Miami? Or how about Africa? Discuss the pluses and minuses of going to one place or another. Then "pretend" to buckle up. "Pretend" the plane is taking off (this involves wiggling in your seat). Pretend the beverage cart comes by, so you can continue drinking your real beer while she picks out what kind of imaginary juice to have. Pretend to hit turbulence and bump into each other (a favorite part). Pretend to see places below, take a nap, and land. Then you can have her go explore what's there, commenting from your window seat. (If you're ready for another beer, you can "explore" by going on a safari where you happen to stumble on an ancient refrigerator that gives forth cold brews, and maybe a juice box . . . then . . . uh-oh! . . . you've angered the locals! Time to mosey back to the plane. . . .)

Then it's time to go home.

If you do this one right, it can stretch out for at least two beers or thirty minutes, whichever comes first.

The Obstacle Course

Throw some pillows on the floor, push the ottoman in front of them, put the can of Lincoln Logs by the door, etc., and make up a "route" where kids jump from pillow to pillow, crawl over the ottoman, jump over the Lincoln Log can and hit the top with their elbow, skip to the kitchen, crawl around the kitchen table, etc. . . . you line the kids up, say, "Ready, set, go!" and then "time" them. If done right, you can sit and read the paper for a good twenty minutes.

NOT QUITE READY FOR THE MINOR LEAGUES

Motor development at this point is such that your child can catch a large ball. This will be an important participation opportunity for you. First, as you've no doubt already acquired many balls of different shapes and sizes, start with a large, soft ball and practice throwing it back and forth. Keep your competitive spirit in check—no spitballs or knuckleballs, please. And remind her to keep her eye on the ball, which of course, is something you'll be telling her for the next twenty years literally, and then the next forty years metaphorically.

A large amount of enthusiasm on your part, played out through your facial expressions and your voice, is easy, and you can't play it up too big. I mean, jeez, she's catching a ball! Who knows where this could all lead?

Once she's mastered the subtleties of catching a ball about the size of a really fat beagle, start working with smaller balls. If she can master something baseball-size, and happens to be able to switch hit, pack up and move to the Dominican

It's important to look like a god to your child, and you should use every cheap trick to achieve this. For example, when she brings a toy doll to you and asks you to fix the arm that has just snapped out of the socket, don't just snap it back in and toss it back to her. Be like, "I don't know if Daddy can fix this . . ." then put your glasses on, fret over it, grunt a few times . . . THEN "magically" fix it. (Dramatically wiping your brow afterward is optional.) In the not too distant future she will be five and asking you to fix some electronic device utilizing nanotechnology. You'll be useless then, so exploit these moments to their fullest potential!

Republic, as their child labor laws are so relaxed that she might be playing for the Memphis Redbirds by the time she's nine.

SARCASM

Yes, you've been sarcastic most of your life. It's the great thing about being you. But it might be wise to remember that sarcasm doesn't work on or around your kid. When you and your buddy Marvin

Kramperknuckle, whom you've known since playing soccer at St. Norbert Parish, get together, sure it can be all "Yeah, *you're* a genius—just like the time you tried to set a record eating White Castles on prom night and blew all over your date" and "I'm so *sure* you could have kicked that field goal from the fifty-two yard line with those girly legs of yours."

Kramperknuckle gets it. But your kid will not.

So when your three-year-old starts asking a lot of questions, resist any temptation to be anything other than sincere. Yes, you'll come in from a February snowstorm completely covered in snow to hear a tiny Cindy Lou Who–type voice say, "Is it snowing outside?"

"Actually it is," is the correct answer. "No, a gigantic bird just pooped on Daddy," is the incorrect answer. Using the latter will lead to, "Really? Can I see it?"

Snide comments of a sarcastic nature are also not healthy. So when you're sitting there and the kid hits his plate in a way that throws food all over him and bonks him in the head, hold off on looking at your wife and saying, "Yeah, he gets that from *your* side of the family." He is developing his language skills rapidly but can't figure out the "joke" of sarcasm. Instead, he will think he's doing something wrong and might end up feeling bad about himself. (Besides, who wants to hear those sarcastic comments come back to haunt you years later when he drops you off at the nursing home?)

Feel free to make the point to your wife when he's out of earshot, though!

Where to Take a Three-Year-Old

Congratulations! You've made it this far, and from here on out, you can pretty much take the kid anywhere save for strip clubs, casinos, the Edward Jones Dome, and other morally questionable places. The good news is you can take him to the ball game—though you won't likely make it through all nine innings, and you'll need to bring a ton of cash because he will want to eat everything. Excessively loud places, like football games and events where there are fireworks, might not work for especially sensitive kids. But as long as you take snacks, coloring books, Matchbox cars, Thomas trains, dolls, and aisle seven of Toys "R" Us, you'll be good!

Oh My Gosh—I Have the Kid for the Day!

The Missouri Botanical Garden seems like more of a place for romantically inclined couples and old people who putter in gardens, but they recently installed a terrific playground. Another fairly recent addition is the Kaeser Maze, which is tons of fun to run around in. Otherwise, the Climatron has been fun for kids to walk through for a couple generations, especially if you pretend it's a magical forest. Of course, there is the tram ride and the huge fish you can feed! But you won't make it through the whole way, and you might want to bring an umbrella stroller or be prepared to carry the kid some of the way. Check for special young children's events, too (www.mobot.org). Also, the Worldways Children's Museum is a great place to spend an afternoon. The exhibits usually explore other cultures and places around the world in fun and interesting ways with a lot of hands-on interactive displays. They often have special events, too (www.worldways.org).

CHAPTER EIGHT
REVIEW QUESTIONS

1. "Children's music" is to "music" what:

    A. "Military intelligence" is to "intelligence"

    B. "River des Peres" is to a "river"

    C. "St. Louis County government" is to "governing"

    D. All of the above

2. Potty training your child is best done:

    A. In winter

    B. When he or she is seven

    C. Drunk

    D. By someone—anyone—but you

3. *Candyland* is (less/more) annoying to play than *Chutes and Ladders*. (Yes, this is a trick question.)

4. Inappropriate or aggressive behavior with others must be dealt with:

    A. Quickly and decisively

    B. Loudly and belligerently

    C. Inconsistently and haphazardly

    D. At the Hooters on Lackland

5. Short Essay: Defend or argue against this statement: "It's just as important to not begin any sentence with, "Oh, yeah, you're a frickin' genius" to your boss or your three-year-old. An extra 10 bonus points if done in iambic pentameter.

When my son Brendan was approaching two years old, he would sit and watch the NBA playoffs with me and I would tell him what a great player Michael Jordan was. A month later, I took him to the Saint Louis University field house to watch some high school teams play. As we crossed the street, I pointed to the huge building and said, "That's a gymnasium." He nodded, showing his understanding. I continued, "They play basketball in there." He nodded again, and excitedly inquired, "Michael Jordan in there?"

—Steve Ehlmann, St. Charles County Executive

Chapter Nine

Four—The Age of "Because I Said So"

Why do we have a home? Why do we eat food? Why do I have to wear pants?

Why can't we have Uncle Bo's car? Why can't our car be red? Why can't we have our neighbor's garage? She has a neat garage. Can I have a lollipop now? Why do you have to go to work?

Why can't I see your belt buckle?

Women think these questions are cute, and they are, for about two minutes. Kids at this age question everything, and believe us when we say: You will be stumped and stumped often. Don't be surprised if you have this exchange:

"Daddy, I want to be a mailman when I grow up. What do you want to be when you grow up?"

If you're stumped, say cowboy or astronaut. Then change the subject quickly.

But the good news, if you and your wife have done your job in the last three years, made it through the toddling and the poopy diapers, and set limits on what they can and can't play with and what they can and can't climb on, then you have earned some important collateral: The get-out-of-jail-free pass of "because I said so."

Feel free to indulge them for a while, just to see where it all goes. Their line of questioning will often lead down roads where you start to answer a simple question like, "What are you doing, daddy?" with "Daddy is doing our taxes."

> HIM: "What are taxes?"
> YOU: "It's money the government takes so we can pay for things."
> HIM: "Like what?"
> YOU: ". . . playgrounds."
> HIM: "Can I take money from you and build playgrounds?"
> YOU: "No."
> HIM: "Why not?"
> YOU: [Drum roll please] "Because I said so."

Didja Know?

At the Magic House, you no doubt noticed the sign that reads, "The average 4 year old asks 437 questions a day." You'll remember fondly the first time you saw that and thought what an exaggeration it must be; now you'll realize it's a gross underestimate. Nay! A gross, *cruel* underestimate.

DINNERTIME CONVERSATION

It's a sacred time, but before you know it you'll find it hard to get the family to sit down together for a meal. Work, sports, homework, school plays, and life in general will get in the way, and everyone will be grabbing a meal or something vaguely resembling one on the run.

Start the dinnertime ritual early on. Eat together without the TV on, and ask each person about his or her day. Now little Claire will likely be in some kind of preschool at this point, if only part time, and even if she's not, she's probably going to find no detail too small or insignificant to relive moment by moment with you. It'll sort of be like talking to your annoying mom, but the responses will be in a higher voice, and not quite so liquored up.

Treat it all as important because it is in her world. Ask a lot of questions, and keep her engaged.

And finally, try to keep her from talking with her mouth full. If the conversation gets too tedious, ask: "So who got in trouble today and what did they do?" That always makes things much more interesting.

LOOK WHAT I CAN DO!

Kids are very impressed with everything they can do. Actively engage them at a suitable level of interest and tone (though don't overdo it), and since they crave their dad's approval, be generous with it.

No matter how inane it all is.

Right Way:

HIM: Look Daddy, look what I can do. I'm touching the coffee table with one hand while I lift up my leg!
DAD: Wow, that is really neat, son. Can you do that with the other hand and the other leg too? You can?!? Well, that's just great.

Not So Right Way:

HIM: Look, Daddy, I can hop on one leg in a circle while I hold this piece of cheese!
DAD: Well lookie-you—mistaking me for someone who gives a rat's butt. Who the hell cares? Anybody can do that. Here's a quarter. Call me when you do something really impressive, like get the governors of Missouri and Illinois to agree on building another bridge from Metro East to downtown! Now that would be somethin' to crow about!

Engaging him when he does this sort of thing (and he will do it a lot) means not just nodding absentmindedly and muttering "uh-huh," but

Like your roommate in college, your four-year-old *loves* it when someone pretends to throw up. So a real thrill is to pretend to eat something, then groan, and proceed to upchuck all over your kid. He'll do it right back at you, and you'll have fun for hours on end. It's educational, too. He learns the importance of comic timing, and how to writhe around on the floor.

To kick it up a notch, actually eat cold White Castles with extra onions. Is the vomiting real? Is it pretend? Only the experts will be able to tell!

watching, then asking him to do something more challenging. Like hopping backwards holding a piece of cracker and spinning a cheese plate on his head. Then you should demonstrate this, ideally in a *tutu*.

THEIR FIRST BIKE

Dads are always in charge of the kid's first bicycling experience. If you're predisposed, you have a good bike that is fitted with a child seat, and you've already taken her for spins on beautiful fall and spring days. You know, the seven of those we get in this town.

Her first two-wheel bike is a special event indeed, and it's likely you or your wife has looked ahead on this and picked up a good, not-too-beat-up one at a garage sale. Your little Evaletta Knievel will need every bit of confidence in leaving the carefree days of "tricycliness" behind and stepping up to the new bike, so you'll instinctively know to make sure the bike is the correct size for her, is in good working order, with the training wheels securely on.

Note: If you are the least bit insecure yourself about your ability to assemble a bike and/or put on training wheels, it's really recommended that you patronize one of the great independent bike stores we have. Yes, you'll pay twenty or forty dollars or

---

Fun Fact!

All those years you spent instilling good manners will likely come back to bite you during this time. So be prepared to hear things like, "Daddy, you're not supposed to talk with your mouth full." Your first instinct will be to shove a heapin' spoon of mashed potatoes in his face and say, "Oh yeah? Well you're not supposed to get a face full of food from a guy who's five times your weight, so there!" and then spit them up all over him adding, "Yeah, last time you try to correct your dad!" Studies show that this is a bad idea.

Creamed corn is better.

---

more than you would at a big box establishment, but it'll come fully and professionally assembled, and best yet, most local independent shops offer free tune up services—something that St. Louisans desperately need as the bike will sit for months in a garage during winter and then need to be cleaned, oiled, and adjusted for her new height. (Make sure you ask about this deal before buying, though.)

Helmet and pads in place, and feeling a little daring, you can forsake your driveway or cul de sac for some of the area's great bike trails. For a list of where to go biking, there are a pair of great sites: www.bikestlouis.org and www.stlbikefed.org, the latter of which also provides a list of the many great independent bike stores we have in the area.

Obviously, you're not going to take the Katy Trail all the way to Booneville or something. But so much of the Katy is flat, you could go a mile or three before stopping for a picnic—a great way to spend the afternoon.

INDEPENDENCE YEAR

During this time he wants to show he is a "big boy" and do a lot of things by himself. Now, at first this seems like a good idea, something you'll welcome, but then you'll find yourself standing in a parking lot for seventeen minutes as he tries to show you how he can open the car door. This is a time for patience, discretion, and more patience.

Lots and lots of patience. Heapin' globs o' patience.

Obviously, from opening a door to putting on shoes to making pancakes, you can step in and do it faster and more efficiently. There will be times when you have to. The trick is to give him the opportunity to do these things (and get better at them) as often as possible. When necessary, offer helpful tips in completing the task.

Right Way:

YOU: That's good you put on your shirt! What a big boy! But usually, they are worn on the top half of you, not the bottom. So consider that for next time! Not that I'm being the least bit critical. I'm being very supportive. You're the best! Despite the fact that, you know, you're wearing your shirt on your butt. Just consider it for next time. That's all I'm sayin'.
HIM: Okay, Dad!

Not So Right Way:

YOU: What the heck are you thinkin' boy? The shirt don't work that way. Do you have poop for brains? Do ya?!?
HIM: I guess I'm not supposed to tell you this, but Mom says my real dad is the UPS guy. Does that make things better or worse? Daddy? Why are you crying? [Pause] Can I have a graham cracker now?

OPINIONS ARE LIKE CARDINALS CAPS—EVERY FOUR-YEAR-OLD HAS ONE

Opinions are another aspect of your little Claire that seem cute, until she starts expressing critical ones aimed at yours truly. At this age, you might think fondly back to when she would simply express what her favorite color was ("My favorite color is red and green and blue and orange and yellow and magenta and red"). But now things are getting sticky. . . .

Be prepared for the four-year-old equivalent of, "You're not going to wear that, are you?" which you're already hearing from your wife. Being a good sport, you have usually "played along" and worn the shirt your wife favors.

Try this with your kid, however, and you are in danger of going down a slippery slope. Giving her too much power will lead to lengthy conversations as she makes you explain why you're taking Manchester with all those stoplights and nary a suicide lane rather than the highway, or why you're investing in a particular mutual fund.

But as a St. Louis dad, it is your duty to challenge certain opinions she might have. We're talking the "I think all boys stink" variety. Engaging her in exploring the issue, as in "Do you really mean *all* or just maybe one in particular who did something today you didn't like?" And as with everything involving conversing with your kid, be wary of saying, "What about Uncle Smitty? You like him and he doesn't stink!" because she will quickly remind you that while he is a nice, fun uncle, to take the statement literally, he does have this odd aroma consisting of an unusual combination of Irish Spring, Sonic double cheeseburgers, and stale PBR.

Still, you'll have made your point. At least, that is, what you'll believe.

QUIET TIME!

Naps are the golden moments of a day, and hopefully you're lucky enough to have a kid who takes them. But even if you are, they are likely long gone by the time they hit four. Moms can tend to just roll over and go with this, but you should consider insisting on "quiet time," at least on the weekends. This is when your furrowed brow, stern voice, and proverbial "putting-down-of-the-foot" come in handy.

Little Albert doesn't have to sleep, but spending an hour quietly in his room is a really good idea for everyone (by "everyone" we mostly mean you and Mom). In a world that overstimulates children with computer games, TV, and your wacky neighbor who never cuts his grass or shaves his face, there is constant pressure for parents to "entertain" their kids. But hearken back to your days of yore and give the boy the same opportunity to just stare out the window for an hour a couple of times a week.

And speaking of great ideas . . . what could you and your wife be doing during that hour? You know, during that so-called "quiet time" . . . hmmm . . . well the gutters always need cleaning. That light switch in the basement needs replacing. Or perhaps that thing you guys did that time that resulted in said kid.

Hey, wouldn't that be different?

GENDER DOESN'T MATTER

Now, as an open-minded St. Louis guy . . . you know, to an extent . . . you may or may not be concerned about some behavior that, well, let's be brutally frank: If you had exhibited similar behavior at

Kennerly Grade School, Lance Bryce would have *really* given you a wedgie before beating you up.

So your little girl hates to wear dresses, always roughhouses, and is always requesting your wife play her Indigo Girls CD. So your little boy shows no interest in anything sports related, even kickball! No, he loves to dance, read stories about princesses, and wears women's clothes so much it would inspire Baton Bob to move back to St. Louis.

Kids are on a long path to finding themselves and appropriately (on an intellectual level anyway) aren't drawing any gender lines or limiting themselves to what they find appealing. So when it's movie night and he wants to watch *Cinderella* again, hold off on saying, "No, that's a girl thing, let's watch *Cars* instead—or better yet, something from my Chuck Norris collection." As much of you'd instinctively want to do this, this is a very happy time in their lives, and to make them start questioning what they like to play with or watch, and to plant ideas in their mind that they could lose your approval simply because they like one toy over another, is really a shame. So buck up.

The exception, of course, is if he suddenly wants to own every Barbra Streisand record. In that case, feel free to overreact, because for anybody under forty, regardless of sex or orientation, damn, that's just *wrong*.

Along these lines, don't limit what you sign the kid up for. First of all, whether it's T-ball or ballet, karate or yoga, the sole point of *any* activity at this age is getting exercise, learning to be in a group setting, and developing social skills. So take her to judo and him to dance class without so much as a blink. The wider variety of activities, the better off he or she will be. And don't just focus on dance, or just on sports.

But regardless of that, there'll be no quitting. At this stage it's good to establish that if they don't care for something, they don't have to sign up for it again, but after two weeks of gymnastics, they can't stop going. They have to at least finish the session. It's an important St. Louis virtue to be the kind of people that finish whatever they start, otherwise they grow up to work for the Missouri State Highway Department. And we're looking at the people who decide to tear up I-40 when I-170 is still in disarray.

THINKING OF NUMBER TWO?

No, this is not about what may or may not be making little Albert smell. We're discussing creating another Albert or Claire. Unless you're completely out-of-control and had one of those "Irish twins" and pretty much got your spouse knocked up right after the first kid, then you possess some restraint and basic math ability, and you should be duly congratulated. But about this time you may enter into a conversation about having more children, or at least a second one.

There are many theories about when to have the next one. A good rule of thumb is you never want to deal with a second one when the first one is still in diapers. If you stick to this rule and are comfortable with your first boy wearing diapers until he's, say, accepted into Wash U's MBA program, then you may have some "issues" about having a second one at all. By all means, be a man and discuss your reluctance with your wife.

Some think the more space there is between one and two, the less chance of them fighting. Forget that. We know of a guy who had three kids, seven years apart, and they fought like crazy.

People have kids for all the wrong reasons. Now that you're child-sensitive, you've seen it at your country club, you've seen it at your trailer park. So don't have a second one because the old lady at the Schnucks berates you for creating a "monster" who is a "spoiled only child." Also, don't have a second one because you're one of eight, and by God, fighting for that stale Twinkie that fell on the floor with seven siblings' elbows in your eyes built your character.

On the one hand, if you have the second one close to the first one, then you get the whole baby thing out of the way at the same time. Then again, if there's too much space between them, they'll both tend to take on first-child characteristics and never be on the same level until they are, say, in their forties.

Bottom line: There's no right answer, though figuring finances, and how you're going to pay for college, is a great idea.

OH MY GOSH—I HAVE THE KID FOR THE DAY!

Two words: City Museum. Sure, it's probably a lawsuit waiting to happen, but where's your sense

You're a reasonable guy, proud of your ability to compromise, but you may be surprised to learn that you can't compromise on the issue of how many kids to have. In other words, you can't have half a baby! If one spouse wants one, and the other is not wild about the notion, the closest thing you can do is say, "Okay, if you have another baby, I get to buy a Triton 197 Magnum fishing boat." (If it's reversed and she's the one who is reluctant, then you can try, "Okay, have the baby, and then I'll buy you a Triton 197 Magnum fishing boat." Get back to us if it works.)

of fun? This is a great place to take a kid—though not too young, as Albert or Claire needs to be old enough to handle the coolness of a three-story slide. Even at four there will be some things he can't do (and if you're over thirty and/or faint of heart, there will be some things you shouldn't do!). This is truly unique to St. Louis, and we're very lucky to have it. What a magical, wonderful place that fires the imagination, inspires the child in all of us, and sells beer (citymuseum.org). If it's one of those beautiful days, an afternoon spent at the Lone Elk Park's World Bird Sanctuary is also pretty cool (worldbirdsanctuary.org).

CHAPTER NINE
REVIEW QUESTIONS

1. On which of the following does "Because I Said So" *not* work?

    A. Your four-year-old

    B. Your dog

    C. Your grandma

    D. Your wife's cat

2. Match the column of people on the left with the activity on the right, for which you must feign genuine over-the-top enthusiasm.

1) Your mother-in-law	a) Doing a somersault on your porch
2) A Belleville cop	b) Only breaking your left kneecap
3) Your kid	c) Staying with you an extra week
4) Your bookie	d) Asking if you're going to finish that donut

3. True/False: A child that regularly has "Quiet Time" is better than a 16-inch Imo's Deluxe.

4. When considering if and when to have a second child, you should:

    A. Consult with your financial adviser

    B. Allow nosy and meddling family and friends to berate you into doing it

    C. Consider adopting someone older, like an eighteen-year-old Swedish girl

    D. Not think about it, just make sure the kid has tons of "quiet time" (wink-wink)

5. Short Essay: Write 500 words on the advantages of having a Triton 197 Magnum fishing boat instead of a four-year-old.

On an October night in 2006, Game 4 of the World Series, my five-year-old son, Cole, already a Cardinal fiend (reading box scores, etc.), was lucky enough to go to the game (bleacher seats) with mom, dad, and little brother. Late in the game, reliever Brad Thompson tossed a ball to him from the bullpen. An older kid intercepted; Thompson shook his finger at that boy, motioning him to give the ball to Cole, which he did. On the way home from the game, Cole, tuckered out from all the excitement, fell into a deep post-game slumber in his car seat. In the rearview mirror, I noticed how "dead" he seemed, his little body lifeless, all his energy spent. Yet there was his hand on his lap still tightly clenching the prize from a time he'll remember always. He still sleeps with ball, along with his little brother.

The following spring, the season began anew, and that little brother, Tad, crawled into bed with mommy and daddy around 2:00 a.m., as is his custom. Before he did, he looked at me and said, "Daddy, I forgot the baseball." His little feet scampered out of the room. Seconds later, he returned, his arm wrapped securely around the ball. There it remained as he climbed into the bed, closed his eyes and dreamed the dreams St. Louis kids dream.

His kids will dream them, too.

—Andy Banker, Fox News

Chapter Ten

Five and Beyond

(...and later we'll turn to the mailbag and answer your questions)

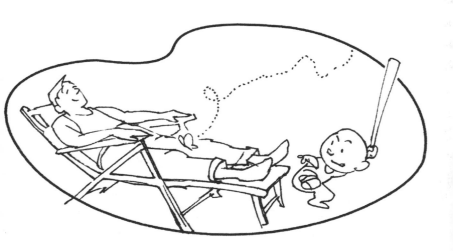

Wow. Five! You are to be congratulated for having such an upstanding, smart, polite, well-behaved, beautiful child. You should also be congratulated because you haven't ended up in a mental health institution, rehab, or as the subject of an investigative report from Fox TV's Chris Hayes. You may breathe easy.

For exactly two minutes.

Okay, we're done with that. No more resting on the proverbial laurels . . . back to dad work.

Now, in the past five years you may have lost some hair, dignity, and semblance of what life was like B.K. (Before Kids). Depending on if and when you pulled the trigger on baby number two, a corner will seem to have been turned when little Albert or Claire turned five. "Seemed" in the sense that . . . well, as one wise St. Louis dad explained it, "It never gets easier; it's always hard—it's just as they go through different stages, there's different stages of 'hard.'"

There's no doubt about it—diapers, stumbling and cracking his head on the coffee table, crying in the middle of the night—that part is (mostly) gone. Now there's real school, sports, and going to the movies together. You can talk to him about important things, as in, "Daddy needs you to be quiet when he watches the news, so go play by yourself for thirty minutes or you won't ever again get any McNuggets."

In most instances, you can reason with him. Consequences and choices are in his intellectual realm. You can all be driving to Chicago for the weekend, and when he announces he has to go to the bathroom, rather than crash through the I-55 guardrail into an open field, you can calmly say, "Do you have to go *now* now, or can you wait twenty minutes until we stop for lunch in Bloomington?"

He's dressing himself. Feeding himself. Riding bikes with you. He's at the ballpark watching the whole game and not getting *too* bored. He's even getting you a beer from the refrigerator. Everything is more "Dad-friendly." And issues like discipline are easier because you've been there for his first five years, and the bond between you and him is stronger than if you had just left all the important child-rearing tasks for your wife to take care of by herself.

So we trust you to take it from here. However, there are a few things you should have a head's up on that aren't necessarily age-specific. . . .

DEATH

Unless you're fortunate, something or someone close to your family may die during your child's first five years. It might be a family pet, a neighbor's pet, a grandparent, a grandparent's neighbor's pet, a neighbor's pet's grandparent, a member of your extended family, or an especially affectionate house plant—something. A young child does not understand the concept of death, so this could be the hardest thing you'll have to handle.

How old the child is, how close she was to the deceased, and your religious convictions are just a few of the variables involved in handling this. But they all have one thing in common: *They all require you to think long and hard before you open your mouth to explain it.*

You're likely grieving, too, so simply telling your child the facts might seem like an option: "Aunt Betty was in a car accident. She crashed in the lake. They took her to the hospital, and then she died." But wow, did you just open up a can of worms. For example, your child might suddenly be completely terrified of cars, water, and hospitals. Six months from now when she falls out of a tree and hurts her arm, and you say, "It's okay, we're going to take you to the hospital," she is likely to recall that when someone goes to the hospital, they are never seen again. So be *very careful* about associating death with doctors or hospitals.

If you tell her something or someone "went to sleep" or was "put to sleep" and "won't ever wake up," that'll pretty much assure that *you* won't be getting sleep for weeks or months as you try to explain to her at bedtime that it's all okay—*she'll* wake up in the morning.

While your religious faith is getting you through this time, consider the consequences of telling someone under five that you're all going to get to see Grandma again someday. She's spent her entire life up to this point just getting her head around the physical world, the world of actions and consequences. So the abstract thought of meeting in the great beyond is beyond little Claire's intellect. If you tell her you'll see Grandma again, don't be surprised if she asks about it six months, a year, three years after the fact, even if you "explained" this when she was only two.

Should she lose someone she was especially close to, seriously consider seeking professional help. It's a fragile time for children, and how this delicate issue is handled can have far-reaching consequences—literally for the rest of her life. In looking for a professional to turn to, you won't find a better source than Psychotherapy Saint Louis (pyschotherapysaintlouis.org). They have many professionals to help during especially challenging times. And please consider putting aside any impulses to "take care of it yourself," as the stakes can be very high.

At the other extreme, if it is Natasha, the old stinky cat your wife brought with her into your marriage, who kicks the bucket, you might have the opposite challenge—being sensitive enough. While your first instinct might be to show the kind of joy one normally associates with finding a great parking spot at Six Flags on a beautiful Saturday morning in June, try to muffle your enthusiasm. Save it for the retelling at poker night.

Regardless, it is recommended that you be firm in conveying that Pillows the hamster or Ada the Grandma is gone. And here's something else that may be comforting: It's okay to tell your child that you don't exactly know. They accept that answer with other things, and they will accept it here. "Spot is gone, and won't be coming back." "Where did he go?" "I'm not exactly sure, honestly. I don't have all the answers. But I do know he liked being here very much and we'll always have our memories of him."

SPORTS—SERIOUSLY

As far as competitive sports goes, it's better to follow Claire's lead in this. Getting her in competitive T-ball at the age of eighteen months is tempting, but probably not useful—for you, her, or anyone else. And when the time comes to get her involved, let's keep your competitive juices in check. Nothing is more obnoxious than a dad who gets red in the face and screams at a coach, a referee, or another parent (and you will see this happen).

Set the tone at the first T-ball game, that it's about teamwork and having fun, and live up to that. Of course, spotting a weakness and working on it early in the backyard is great as long as it's done with the idea that the better one gets at something, the more fun it usually is. Resist putting any kind of pressure on her, or letting her think that if she doesn't meet certain expectations, she'll disappoint you.

If she shows an amazing talent right out of the womb for sports and can't get enough of them, you'll find yourself excited and supporting her all the way, which is great—to a point. Even young children can get burnt out and never want to participate in that sport or any other game again. Make sure she's not putting too much pressure on herself, and also work to get balance in her life. Too much of one thing is not good.

Also, don't panic if by five she's shown no interest in sports . . . as long as she is interested in *something*, like dance, gymnastics, music, or anything that requires working with others for a common goal. If by five she's displaying an unusual penchant for bunko, then you might raise an eyebrow and discourage her until, you know, she's like eighty.

THE COLLEGE FUND

Speaking of college, you have a fund set up already, right? You're putting something away every month, right? (Buying a cute little "Mizzou Tigers" pajama outfit with the little footsies *does not* count as an "investment" in her college education.)

Consider designating yourself the long-term-thinking member of Team Baby. Now, schoolin'-wise, your immediate hope is to see him graduate from PTU (Potty Training University). But you can't start too soon on setting up a college fund. Sure, you're a Dad, and it's perfectly fine to figure in that full basketball scholarship to Mizzou . . . still, let's also be working on a plan "B."

No matter how broke you are, start a college fund as soon as possible, even if it's ten dollars a month. Missouri colleges and universities' yearly tuition increases have been the highest in the country, and in 2007, the University of Illinois in Springfield was mulling over a 13.9 percent increase. Statistically, across the nation it costs $12,000 to $20,000 total *now* to get a college education, and if you're reading this and your kid is five, it could be as high as $130,147 when they graduate! And that's for an in-state public university (source: www.smartmoney.com/college/investing).

Of course the cost of *not* having a college education is even more expensive—just ask the forty-two-year-old barista at the local Starbucks.

There are many ways to set up a fund. It can be as simple as a separate savings account at the bank (but have the discipline to *never* touch it). Some employers offer plans, and your friendly neighborhood financial specialist or broker will certainly have a lot of plans. But starting something early is best.

And here's another tip: You know all the tons of crap that he gets for birthdays, Christmas, and "just because" dates? Try to get members of your family to give money for the college fund or, better yet, U.S. savings bonds to be used for college. It's so much better than yet another stuffed Mickey Mouse.

A ND NOW YOUR QUESTIONS ...

You've all been calling and writing in with questions, queries, and comments. We appreciate the ones written on paper or sent via email, but whoever sent one scrawled on a dirty diaper, well, *that was not funny at all.*

So instead of a test, you can put your number two pencils down and read from the mailbag with us.

Dear STLD:
Now that I have young children, I look at Halloween completely differently. It used to just be an excuse to get drunk in Soulard. Now, I walk around the neighborhood with my toddler and we get a load of candy. Good stuff, too—Snickers bars, M&Ms, not the lame stuff I got when I was a kid, like Necco wafers or Smarties. But here's the thing: I feel that to let my boy eat all this candy would be completely irresponsible, yet I feel guilty for eating most of it, as much as I enjoy it. What should I do?
—Tom in Tower Grove

Dear Dad in Tower Grove:

Stop feeling guilty! Your son should be grateful to have such a caring dad who will eat most of his candy, while he only gets no more than one piece a day for the first week, and then after, maybe one piece a week (if there's any left).

And Tom, this actually also goes for those birthday party gift bags he'll bring home. Go through that stuff, and selectively "prune" those, too. Since he can't count, he won't really know, and with the money you'll save years later on dentist bills, you can buy him some broccoli or something. However, don't elbow him out of the way to get to the stuff that falls out of the piñata.

Dear STLD:

Here's the problem with Christmas: When I talk up Santa with my little girl, I'm overcome by the fact that I'm telling her a big fat lie. When the day comes that she figures it out, I feel my credibility as a Dad will be severely damaged—I mean, I imagine her thinking, "If he lied to me about this, maybe he's lying to me about when construction on Highway 40 will finally be completed." Yet the alternative seems too extreme: That Santa is only a character like FredBird. What do I do?

—Jerry in Jennings

Dear Dad in Jennings:

Yes, you are feeding your precious little girl a big fat lie. Yet Christmas is a special time in St. Louis, so you can't take that away from her. So we recommend taking a stance of "plausible deniability." Let your *wife* feed her the biggest portion of the lie, and you support the whole idea by taking a backseat on the issue.

As she gets older, maybe even by four, she'll notice that she is seeing a lot of Santas around. If she's especially perceptive, she'll notice that they are different and ask you awkward questions like, "Daddy, why does the breath on the Santa at Chesterfield Mall smell like Natural Light, while the breath on the Santa at the Galleria smells more like a Stone Hill Norton, perhaps the 2004 vintage?" Then you might consider explaining that those mall Santas are the real Santa's "helpers" because he's too busy at the North Pole to fly into a parking lot at the Mills on a Saturday.

While we're on the subject, though, one word of caution: Your wife will probably want to make this all a bigger deal than the young child can handle. If you think about it, a big fat guy that's not your brother Dwayne coming down the chimney in the middle of the night . . . well, it's a little scary. Some kids freak out about it, especially the whole being-forced-to-sit-on-his-lap-at-the-mall thing. Also, we recommend you not use Santa as a weapon as in, "If you don't pick up your Little People right now, we'll tell Santa and you won't get any presents." This will usually backfire, one way or another.

Dear STLD:

I've been married for six years and we have a daughter who just turned two. Thing is, I'm really unhappy about it all. My wife nags me all the time, I don't get to go drinking with my buddies every night like I used to, the kid cries a lot. It's just a drag and I'm thinking of

leaving and getting a divorce—you know, to reclaim my
former self. That's cool to do, right?

—Fred in Fairview Heights

Dear Dad in Fairview Heights:
Sure! If it's all turning into a drag you can
absolutely abandon everyone . . . in eighteen years.
Until then, shut up and deal with it. See, it stopped
being about you the second your daughter was born.
Now you're a Dad first, and all decisions need to be
based on what is best for the kid. What is decidedly
not best for the kid is if the Dad leaves, especially
during the first five years. It's the critical time for
development, and divorce causes an undue and
unfair amount of damage to an innocent kid. It's
really only something total scums do, so buck up,
shut up, and ask your wife nicely if you can have a
once-a-month poker game and join a bowling league
with your loser friends who still live with their
parents. Use those few hours a month to "reclaim
your former self."

Dear STLD:
Every time my two-year-old boy is given some big,
expensive toy, especially something I have to spend hours
assembling, all he wants to do is play with the box. The
cooler the toy, the more he ignores it in favor of the
cardboard. Now, his third birthday is coming up and
I'm thinking of just giving him a bunch of boxes, and
with the money I save, buying a new putter. What do you
think?

—Barney in Barnhart

Dear Dad in Barnhart:

Alas, while making perfect sense, your plan won't work. If you haven't figured it out already, using logic with kids under five is completely futile. I'm afraid he'll just look inside the empty box and burst into tears. But here's one thing you might try: Buy that putter you're eyeing, attach some lights and things that make goofy sounds, put *that* in a big box, and give it to him. See if that works!

Dear STLD:

Is there a difference between indulging your kid and spoiling him? If so, what is it?

—Homer in Hanley Hills

Dear Dad in Hanley Hills:

"Indulging" is what you do as a wise and benevolent father. "Spoiling" is what that jerk across the street who makes more money than you do does to his brat. Good for nothing . . . and why does he wait so long to bring his trash cans back from the curb when it's clearly past the neighborhood association's mandated time? Don't get us started.

Dear STLD:

How much television is too much for a child under five?

—Flanders in Ferguson

Dear Dad in Ferguson:

There is a simple equation:

Mom + any TV with kid = neglect.
Dad + any TV with kid = "quality time."

You see, Mom will try to "use" TV as an opportunity to clean the house, bathe, or something that leads to making dinner. (Duh! That's why Racanelli's is programmed into the phone!) But *you* are doing serious bonding, whether you're snoring to the sounds of the Disney Channel or giving him your own play-by-play as the Rams try to move the ball down the field four yards at a time.

Important to this equation is periodically saying, "You watch too much TV" and "You won't tell Mom about this, right?" Then you'll be generally okay.

Also, randomly, take him outside and throw the football around for a few moments during a commercial.

Dear STLD:

In the morning when my wife and I are getting ready for work and getting our little girl dressed, all sharing a tiny bathroom, at some point we're all naked. I never thought about this when she was two or three but now that she's getting four or five . . . at what point should kids stop seeing their parents naked?

—Mickey in Manchester

Dear Dad in Manchester:

Excellent question. We encourage all St. Louis adults to feel shame for their naked self, and as anyone who has seen an inappropriately revealing tube top at Strassenfest will agree, there's too much collective skin showing in this town. There is a desperate need for more modesty, and it should begin at home.

Certainly by the time your kid hits five, exposure to the nudity of the parent of the opposite sex should cease, lest you find yourself explaining that Mark McGwire image you had tattooed on your butt in 1998. Buy some robes at Dillard's, for cryin' out loud.

Dear STLD:

I just can't believe how wonderful my little girl is. I hear other Dads say these kinda things, but I am absolutely convinced she is the most beautiful, smartest, most amazing little girl on the planet. Am I right?

— Donald of Des Peres

Dear Dad in Des Peres:

You're absolutely right.

APPENDIX A
ARE YOU SAHD MATERIAL?

You've thought of some pretty outrageous things in your life: Trying out for the Billikens, applying to be a taster at Anheuser-Busch, taking Manchester to anywhere.

But here's the thing: If you can just open your mind a bit, being a Stay At Home Dad (SAHD) is a worthy consideration. (The term "Full Time Dad" is also used.) One of the problems with our society is while there's a lot of lip service given to the family and the importance of children, the federal and state government and the vast majority of corporations don't mean it enough to structure the work environment in a way that allows for the raising of children to *come first*. So it's up to Team Baby, the parents, to do some critical soul-searching and really put the kid first. That process might reveal some interesting options. . . .

Everyone agrees that it's best if the Mom stays home with the kids. But what if *Dad* can stay at home with the kids? It's an idea that is not even considered or explored about 99.99994 percent of the time—but there's a small and growing number of men in St. Louis who have taken up the gauntlet and become the primary caregiver for the betterment of their children.

They just don't like to talk about it.

When It Should Be Considered

Some combination of the following variables makes it possible to even consider this bold but important option:

1. She brings home more bacon. Maybe she's a lawyer, a corporate executive, or a field goal kicker for the Rams. You can get by on just one income, and since hers is bigger, using basic math, you figure that yours is the one to go. Boom. You're SAHD.

2. She loves her job. You? Not so much. Can't stand your job? It's going nowhere? Think your boss is a total jerk?

Feel that if your cubical mate says, "Different Day, Same S***" one more time you'll be doing forty-fifty years in the Missouri State Pen for homicide? Why don't you show all of those losers by taking on a much better position—putting your baby first. Success is the *second* sweetest revenge; the first is proving you have your priorities straight.

3. Meet Your New Boss: You. For the vast majority of us, getting by on just one income is too much of a hardship—but what about one and a half? If you're fortunate to have skills that allow for freelance or independent contract work (computers, accounting, contracting, public relations, marketing, etc.), this could be your chance to lay that foundation that will one day allow you to have your own business.

4. No Foolin', More Schoolin'. Since about your second day as an IT manager for a major accounting firm, you've known that the last thing on this earth you were cut out to be was an IT manager at a major accounting firm. This whole baby thing could be your ticket out of there. A part-time job (or not), plus night school, and *voila!* By the time the kid is ready for kindergarten, you're a professional landscaper/small business owner/belly dancer.

Really What It's Like

It's hard, sure. And not in a good way. But a Dad who stays home brings a different dynamic to the whole family thing. You're completely capable, and you get blank stares at cocktail parties when you try to describe what you do. For the most important person on the planet, however—your little boy or girl—it's an opportunity to grow up differently.

You appreciate what your Mom did for you, and yet you're grateful someone, even you, is fortunate to stay at home with the baby/toddler/little boy. It's not flattering to the ego, but it's immensely rewarding, especially in the long term.

It's a bit lonely. You'll eventually meet a few other full-time dads, though most likely you'll find yourself just becoming friends with the "cooler" Moms in the playgroups, story times, and parks. Speaking of which, it takes a bit of a stiff upper lip to be hanging out at the park with your toddler on a weekday morning.

"With other moms at the park, it's all 'Awww—a mother with her baby!'" local comedian Craig Hawksley said in a *St. Louis Magazine* article on the subject. "But if a man shows up, it's 'Bum! Can't hold a job,' or it's 'He must be divorced because he's a bad husband.' [Guys] get no credit for this." Hawksley was a SAHD long before there was even a term for it.

It can be tedious—but so can the monthly staff meeting. And the SAHD has to be particularly vigilant in terms of taking care of himself. If there's no part-time work or school, then he needs to have weekly outings with the buddies to maintain some sort of equilibrium.

But no one is better suited to take care of your newborn than his parent. Whatever sacrifices can be made to accomplish this, little Albert will thank you for it. (In his own special way—like spitting up on you all the time . . . but you'll know what he means by it.)

Support

Statistics are in short supply, but the U.S. Census reports about 100,000 SAHDs. That number is most likely a gross underestimation. For example, when the census counts a Mom who happens to work part-time or does some work outside of her home, she's counted as a "stay-at-home Mom." A man in the exact same situation is counted as "underemployed!"

Other cities have organized groups of SAHDs, but there does not seem to be an organized one here in St. Louis, yet. A great source of information and support is www.rebeldad.com. On that site is a list of blogs by dads, articles, rantings, and guidelines on forming your own Dads group. There is also www.athomedad.com (motto: "Men who change diapers change the world").

The biggest support will come from within, however. It'll be the hardest job you'll not always love, but a sacrifice that will more than pay off in the well-being of your child.

And yes, you can still wear pants while doing it.

Appendix B
Especially Dad-Friendly Things
to Do with Kids under 5

Those who have traveled or have lived elsewhere can heartily confirm what those less worldly instinctively know: We live in an amazing, wonderful city to raise a family. We have world-class institutions dedicated to children that easily top the similar attractions of bigger cities. The best part is that many of them are free.

Compiled here are those places that St. Louis dads with kids under five are known to particularly enjoy. No doubt we've missed some—and perhaps you might disagree with some of our recommendations. In either case, we'd like to hear from you for the next edition of the book: Please email us at books@reedypress.com.

Grant's Farm

1001 Gravois Road **South County**
314.843.1700 **www.grantsfarm.com**

Open: Spring: mid-April to mid-May, Wednesday–Friday, 9 a.m. to 3 p.m.; Saturday, 9 a.m. to 3:30 p.m.; Sunday, 9:30 a.m. to 3:30 p.m. Summer: mid-May to mid-August, Tuesday–Friday, 9 a.m. to 3:30 p.m.; Saturday, 9 a.m. to 4 p.m.; Sunday, 9:30 a.m. to 4 p.m.

Cost: "Free" (But parking is $8 per vehicle, and there's really no where else to park.)

On the dad-friendliness chart, this small animal park ranks about a 12 on a scale of 1–10. First, it's fairly small and you can do it in 90 minutes, and second, what part of "FREE BEER" can you not understand?

Children get to bottle feed the goats, but be warned: Later in the season, the goats get especially aggressive and can freak out the younger kids. But even then you can have your toddler feed the goats through the fence.

Fun Facts: In the 1960s and 1970s, it served an unlimited amount of free beer to adults!

Membership: For $30 you can purchase a parking pass, which is a deal if you go four times or more a season. Especially if you live in the South/West County and South City areas, we say: **Worth It**.

Magic House

516 Kirkwood Road **Kirkwood**
314.822.8900 **www.magichouse.org**

Open: Labor Day to Memorial Day: Tuesday–Thursday, 12 p.m. to 5:30 p.m.; Friday, 12:00 p.m. to 9 p.m.; Saturday, 9:30 a.m. to 5:30 p.m.; Sunday, 11 a.m. to 5:30 p.m. Memorial Day to Labor Day: Monday, Wednesday, Thursday, & Saturday, 9:30 a.m. to 5:30 p.m.; Tuesday & Friday, 9:30 a.m. to 9 p.m.; Sunday, 11 a.m. to 5:30 p.m.

Cost: $7.50, children under 2 are free. Free on the third Friday of every month from 5:30 p.m. to 9 p.m. (but boy does it get crowded then).

Zagat Survey named this St. Louis gem the "number one national attraction for childhood appeal." To put it into perspective, this hands-on interactive museum beat out Disney World. And now it's about to expand. A very dad-friendly place, it's easy to watch toddlers and babies crawl around in their own special section, and with the slightly older kids, you can build something in the construction area and go "fishing."

Membership: The basic membership at $60, while a little restrictive, is a great value. We say: **Definitely Worth It.**

St. Louis Zoo

One Government Drive **Forest Park, St. Louis**
314.781.0900 **www.stlzoo.org**

Open: Every day except Christmas and New Year's Day. Summer: May 25–September 3, 8 a.m. to 7 p.m.; rest of the year: 9 a.m. to 5 p.m. (Note: always check the website or call though—they close the park occasionally or shorten their hours for special events.)

Cost: Free

Of course, you're already familiar with our world-class zoo, as it is one of the crown jewels of St. Louis. But a few dad-specific comments are necessary. It is another attraction that is "free," although parking is $10 per vehicle. But there is free parking available along the street. For this and many other reasons, we advise dads to show some discipline and get there right when it opens, first thing in the morning, for best results. When you do, parking, crowds, and the heat are not a problem. Now, once you're inside, there are a bunch of hidden costs: $4 for the Children's Zoo, $2 for the carousel, $5 for the Zooline Railroad, and $3 for the Sea Lion Show—all of which are especially popular with the 3 to 5 set. For the first hour of operation every day, the Children's Zoo and carousel are free.

Fun Fact: There are five thousand animals in the zoo, and as you may or may not remember from high school biology, they mostly all reproduce sexually. So there's a chance that you might expose your child to some sort of coupling that you'd rather not explain right then and there. Should that happen, just move quickly to where the two-toed sloths are. They rarely do anything.

Membership: For $80 you can get a family pass. It includes passes to all the features that cost money, free parking for six visits, and various other things you probably won't use. We say: **Not Worth It.**

The City Museum

701 N. 15th Street   **St. Louis**
314.280.9214   **www.citymuseum.org**

Open: Every day but Easter, Thanksgiving, and Christmas Day. Monday–Thursday, 9 a.m. to 5 p.m.; Friday, 9 a.m. to 1 a.m.; Saturday, 10 a.m. to 1 a.m.; Sunday, 11 a.m. to 5 p.m.

Cost: $12 for all, kids under 3 free (add $6 admission to attached World Aquarium)

St. Louisans in the know are grateful to internationally known artist Bob Cassilly, who has given us one of the most odd, unusual, and imaginative places on the planet, let alone this town. It is, however, the opposite of "free"—it's actually fairly pricey by St. Louis standards and definitely not worth it for the dad with a kid under three. Otherwise, it's exceptionally dad-friendly (the fact that you can get a cold Schlafly's is just one reason). The dad who is still a kid himself (and who of us isn't?) will marvel at the place; the missus will think it's a lawsuit waiting to happen. But once you take your kid down the three-story slide, swing on the ropes, and explore the unusual tunnels, you'll be hooked.

Fun Facts: It's housed in the 600,000-square-foot former International Shoe Company building, and everything in it is found objects—there's nothing "new" about it.

Membership: If you thought the admission was pricey, then you'll likely recoil at the membership fees, which begin at $200 and go up to $500. Unless you're Moneybags Malone and/or live in a nearby loft, we must say: **Not Worth It.**

Saint Louis Science Center

5050 Oakland Avenue   **St. Louis**
314.289.4400   **www.slsc.org**

Open: Monday–Thursday, 9:30 a.m. to 4:30 p.m; Friday, 9:30 a.m. to 9:30 p.m., Saturday, 9:30 a.m. to 4:30 p.m; Sunday, 11:30 a.m. to 4:30 p.m.

Cost: Free, but charge for special exhibits and $3 for the Discovery Room

Another St. Louis attraction with "free" admission but steep parking: $8. There is free parking at the Planetarium in Forest Park, but you have to arrive early to get it. The Discovery Room is fun but nothing new if you have a train table or dress-up clothes at home. The OMNIMAX has the capacity to freak out some young ones, but some take to the spectacle better than their bottle. Speaking of freaking out, the giant T-rex you encounter as soon as you walk in can offer up differing opinions to kids under five. There are a lot of fun hands-on exhibits and even special presentations that the under-five crowd loves. The Science Center is more of an attraction that your kid will grow into, but it's also a place that, if you pay attention, you may learn a thing or two from as well.

Fun Fact: The walkway over Highway 40 is the coolest part of the center, clocking cars' speed and providing opportunities to moon motorists.

Membership: $75 for families. If you use the Discovery Room, park in the lot, and go to the OMNIMAX, you'll get your money's worth, as free passes are part of the membership. The amount of OMNIMAX tickets you receive alone makes the family membership a value. We say: **Worth It**.

The Gateway Arch

Downtown riverfront   **St. Louis**
314.655.1700   **www.gatewayarch.org**

Open: Winter: 9 a.m. to 6 p.m.; Summer: 8 a.m. to 10 p.m.

Cost: Adults $10, Children 3–12, $3; plus parking in the nearby garage which varies in price and is sometimes free

While it visually defines our fine city, you'd be surprised how many locals forget to *go* to the Arch. In addition to the thrilling/scary ride up in those tiny egg-shaped trams, there is a wonderful museum on westward expansion, which, while potentially not great for kids under three, older and more mature kids will get a kick out of it. If you're down there with the fam and it's a nice day, rent a quadcycle and bike around.

Fun Fact: The Arch weighs 17,246 tons, and 900 tons of stainless steel were used to build it, more than any other project in history, so don't try to move it.

Missouri Botanical Garden

4344 Shaw   **St. Louis**
314.577.5100   **www.mobot.org**

Open: 9 a.m. to 5 p.m.; until 8 p.m. in the summer on Wednesdays

Cost: $4, Kids under 12 free; Children's Garden Playground $3 per child, adults and kids under 2 free

This decidedly chick place has gotten more dad- and kid-friendly lately, especially since the Children's Garden Playground was put in. Make sure you chase your tyke through the cool Kaeser Maze, ride on the tram, and walk through the Climatron (pretend it's a jungle and you're African explorers looking for exotic rare birds and old ladies with blue hair). Finally, with your pockets stuffed with coins, head to the Japanese garden to feed the huge koi fish.

Fun Fact: Several of the huge fish bare a striking resemblance to your wife's favorite gapped-tooth cousin, Sanford. But whether you point this out to your son or daughter is left up to your discretion.

Membership: $150 for families. With each visit, you get to bring up to ten guests for free, but you will still have to pay for the Children's Garden after your young one turns two. Also, even with membership, you still pay a discounted admission for some special events. Unless you go steadily, we say: **Not Worth It**.

Laumeier Sculpture Park

12580 Rott Road   **South County**
314.821.1209   **www.co.st-louis.mo.us/parks/laumeier**

Cost: Free

Not your traditional park, this gem is a ninety-eight-acre open-air museum filled with modern art, most of which may lead you to scratch your head and say, "Hey! I could have done that!" (Note: But you didn't, at least not first.) The main part of the park with the big metal art things reaching into the sky is cool, sure, but what's especially dad-friendly is the trail located just north of the parking lot. It's heavily shaded and is great on hot days, especially in the morning. Along the trail you will find art to climb on, run through, and best of all, make up stories about. Plus, you can take the dog! (Note: one drag is the trail isn't that suitable for strollers, so either wear your baby in a carrier or make sure your kid can walk a short trail.)

Fun Fact: There's a sculpture there that looks like a giant metal egg. Ask your kid to imagine the size of the chicken that laid it.

Museum of Transportation

3015 Barrett Station Road   **St. Louis**
314.965.7998   **www.museumoftransport.org**

Open: Labor Day–April 30: Tuesday to Saturday, 9 a.m. to 4 p.m.; Sunday, 11 a.m. to 4 p.m.; May 1–Labor Day: Monday, Wednesday, Friday, & Saturday, 9 a.m. to 5 p.m.; Thursday, 9 a.m. to 7 p.m.; Sunday, 11 a.m. to 5 p.m.

Cost: Children $2, adults $4, Creation Station $1.50

The 70-plus locomotives won't be as cool to your young'in as they'll likely be to you, but the cars and planes, and the ride on the one-mile miniature train by 24-inch scale replicas of the 1863 C.P. Huntington steam locomotion is cool. Now for a couple of extra bucks, the toddler and young child can have loads of fun in the Creation Station playroom, which we strongly recommend. Also, in the summer they host special storytime events.

Fun Fact: The Earl C. Lindburg Automotive Center includes Bobby Darin's infamous "Dream Car" designed by Andy DiDia in 1953, costing more than $93,000 and taking seven years to build . . . well, it's way cool.

Membership: A membership for a year is a mere $40, and if you live in the area and can get there regularly in under 30 minutes, it's **Worth It**.

St. Louis Mills Mall

5555 St. Louis Mills Boulevard   **Hazelwood**
314.227.5555   **www.stlouismills.com**

I know—a mall? But not just any mall, an especially friendly mall for Dads and their kids under five. They have two indoor playgrounds: One for bigger kids, one for little. Nearby is a toy store with a train table (there's also a train table in the bookstore on the other side of the mall). An especially good destination on cold, rainy, or excessively hot days, Dad can get a coffee or a shake and hang out, then stroll around and get some shopping done . . . or better yet, catch the Blues practicing.

Fun Fact: Local PBS station KETC often hosts special events there, like a reading program.

Worldways Children's Museum

15479 Clayton Road   **Ballwin**
636.207.7405   **www.worldways.org**

Open: Monday–Saturday, 9 a.m. to 5:30 pm.; Sunday, 12 p.m. to 5:30 p.m.

Cost: $5 for everyone

This is a fun, educational way to spend an hour or so with your four and five year old. Interactive displays help your growing boy or girl learn that there is a world outside St. Louis. Clothes from other countries are there for dress up, as are games from other cultures (nary a *Candyland* to be found). You can pretend to make things like tortillas, and it's a great bridge to eating later at a Mexican place that doesn't have a playground, but does serve margaritas.

Fun Fact: There's a fun exhibit about one of St. Louis's sister cities, Saint-Louis, Senegal, from which you'll learn fascinating things, including that there is such a thing as "sister cities."

Edwardsville Children's Museum

722 Holyoake Road   **Edwardsville, IL**
618.692.2094   **www.childrens-museum.net**

Open: Tuesday, Friday, & Saturday, 10 a.m. to 3:30 p.m.

Cost: $3

This is generally geared toward older kids, though certainly the three to five crowd will enjoy playing in the dress-up area at the very least. Kids can also see themselves on the TV screen as they play reporter in the television "newsroom." (Sit them down and have them make up something about what the weather will be, and if they are wildly wrong, maybe they can grow up to be a local weather reporter!) Building forts out of the PVC pipe is also a lot of fun.

Fun Fact: In the fall, they host a carnival where local businesses get involved in the act and do their own take on interactive fun.

Whittle Train Store

24 Front Street   Valley Park
636.861.3334   www.woodentrain.com

Open: Tuesday–Friday, 10 a.m. to 4 p.m., Saturday, 9 a.m. to 5 p.m.; Sunday, 12 p.m. to 5 p.m.

Cost: Free

If your kid is into toy trains, man, is this a great place to visit. You'll find huge train tables with exquisitely built "cities" and lots of toys for them to look at (but, no, Daddy isn't going to buy you another Thomas train today). They sell coffee, soda, and snacks and provide tables, so bring a paper and relax and watch your kids become mesmerized by the trains.

Fun Facts: Legend has it the place was a house of ill repute in the 1800s, and if you listen closely enough you can almost hear the dance hall music. It's located across the street from an actual train track, so usually during one's stay all the kids run to the windows to watch the real train before they go back to putting the little trains in their mouths.

Faust Park

15185 Olive   Chesterfield
636.537.0222   www.co.st-louis.mo/us/parks/faust

Butterfly House Hours: Memorial Day to Labor Day, 9 a.m. to 5 p.m., seven days a week; Rest of the year: 9 a.m. to 4 p.m. Tuesday–Sunday

Butterfly House Cost: $6 adults, $4 children 4–12, and Free for children under 3

One of our city's most beautiful parks, Faust has a carousel that you and your little one can go for a spin on for a buck. There is also a historical village where you can walk with your inquisitive youngster and make stuff up—like how you remember growing up churning your own butter. And finally, there's the beloved Butterfly House, which all kids love— unless they are scared of things flying around them, and some of the more sensitive tots are. Faust also has a new playground that is swell.

Fun Fact: The carousel was installed in 1929 at the Forest

Park Highlands, and when the Highlands burned down in 1963, it was the only thing left standing. It was dismantled and taken to Sylvan Spring Park from 1965 until 1980. It was then restored and installed in Faust in 1987.

Powder Valley Conservation Nature Center

11715 Cragwold Road   **Kirkwood**
314. 301.1500   **mdc.mo.gov/areas/cnc/powder**

Open: Year round, 8 a.m. to 5 p.m.

Cost: Free

Powder Valley is perfect for people who like to think they're "hiking" but can only handle a mile on a paved surface. Even with those amenities (there are longer trails too), you feel like you're out in the wild with deer and other critters frolicking nearby. With a thick canopy of shade, it's perfect for those hot summer days. Inside the center is an aquarium and neat kid-friendly exhibits (puppet theater and treehouse), some newly revamped. Powder Valley also hosts informational talks and a monthly story time.

Lone Elk Park

1 Lone Elk Park Road   **Valley Park**
314.615.7275   **www.co.st-louis.mo.us/parks/LoneElk**

Open: Daily, 7:30 a.m. to sunset; closed Christmas

Cost: Free

Picnic with the bison, elk, deer, ducks, and turkeys, then cross the road to the World Bird Sanctuary. If your kid is young enough to wear (as in a bjorn), you can walk the four-mile Bison Trail, and he or she will love it. For kids that are walking, going just a little ways on the trial and walking back is recommended. Note: Leave Fido at home—apparently dogs and large mammals with horns don't always mix.

Dental Health Theatre

727 N. First Street, Suite 103 **Laclede's Landing**
314.241.7391

Open: Monday–Friday, 9 a.m. to 3 p.m.; shows are 45 minutes long

Cost: Free (But they only do shows for groups of 15 or more, so call and ask if there is a group you can tag along with or if they are reasonably sure they'll get enough visitors that day)

This one-of-its-kind in the world (for obvious reasons!) offers sixteen illuminated three-foot-long teeth properly placed on a pink-carpeted lower gum. Presentations are forty-five minutes long and include two short films and a marionette show. Now, we know what you're thinking—I'm going to take my kid to a demonstration about flossing? But young kids love it, and they do learn something.

Fun Fact: A Chicago dentist created these Godzilla-like chompers in the 1970s, and a local dentist bought them and brought them here to the River City.

Purina Farms

200 Checkerboard Square **Gray Summit**
314.982.3232 **www.purinafarms.com**

Open: Memorial Day–Labor Day: Tuesday–Sunday with reservations, 9:30 a.m. to 3 p.m.

Cost: Free, but reservations are required. Sometimes a small fee for special events.

If your kid loves animals, this is a fun place to visit. Some of the hands-on exhibits are a bit lame (want to learn how pet food is made, anyone?), but they have a barn where kids can go through tunnels, swing on ropes, and pet baby animals such as chickens, ducks, goats, and rabbits. There's an outside maze and a tractor pulling a wagon for rides. Of course, there are also dogs and cats and a dog show that, again, won't keep you spellbound but is a fun distraction for the little one.

Suson Park

6059 Wells Road   **South County**
314.615.4386   **www.stlouisco.com/parks/suson.html**

Open: April through September: 10:30 a.m. to 5 p.m. daily;
October through March: 10:30 a.m. to 3:00 p.m. daily

Cost: Free

This great spot has an animal farm with lots of horses, cows,
goats, chickens, and pigs. A couple of really nice small lakes
that are stocked every three weeks make it a great spot for the
burgeoning fisher-person. Be warned: The inferior playground
requires socks and shoes as the ground consists of the dreaded
little rocks, and the equipment is all 1960s-style metal and not
friendly to toddlers at all. Still, the good outweighs the bad,
and it's worth a trip.

Forest Park Boathouse

6101 Government Drive   **St. Louis**
314.367.2224   **stlouis.missouri.org/citygov/parks/**
forestpark/boathouse

Open: Monday–Saturday, 11 a.m. to 9 p.m.; Sunday, 10 a.m. to
9 p.m.

Paddleboat and Rowboat Cost: $15 per hour

The Boathouse is a fun addition to Forest Park and perfect
to take your three to five year old for a little spin around the
lake. If you go on a Sunday, you'll likely also get to hear some
live music. Consider going to the new inclusive Wonderland
playground in the park, then taking a little boat ride; by
then your little apple of your eye should be calm enough to
sit for a snack at the restaurant while you enjoy a glass of
wine! (Warning: the quality of service is spotty and can be
notoriously slow. Pack a bunch of crackers.)

Life Christian Church's Woody's Café

13001 Gravois Road　　　　　　　　　　**South County**
www.lifechristian.net

Open: Most weekends and after school

Cost: Free

The good people at Life Christian Church have created a terrific play area in Woody's Café, a great indoor place for a dad to take his kid to have fun and burn off some energy. This larger-than-life indoor playground is better than any McDonalds, plus you can get pizza or a cup of coffee (and much more).

Bounce U

Chesterfield & South County　　　　　**Chesterfield:**
　　　　　　　　　　　　　　　　　　　　636.522.5867
www.bounceu.com　　　　　　　　　　**South County:**
　　　　　　　　　　　　　　　　　　　　314.845.7529

Open: Open Bounce and Preschool Playdate times vary

Cost: $6.95; Free for Adults accompanied by child

This is a decent place for a dad to kill an hour with his kid. They have specific preschool playdates for ages 2 to 6 on Tuesdays and Thursdays, which is good when you find yourself with your little boy or girl on a weekday, especially on rainy, cold, or especially hot days. Wears 'em out, too!

SkyZone Recreational Center

17379 Edison Avenue　　　　　　　　**Chesterfield**
636.530.4550　　　　　　　**www.skyzonesports.com**

Open Jump Hours: Summer: Sunday–Tuesday, 12 p.m. to 10 p.m.; Wednesday–Saturday, 10 a.m. to 10 p.m.; Regular hours: Mondays: closed; Tuesday–Thursday, 3 p.m. to 8 p.m.; Friday, 12 p.m. to 10 p.m.; Saturday, 10 a.m. to 10 p.m.; Sunday, 10 a.m. to 8 p.m.

Cost: $10 per hour, monthly jump membership $45 (limited to Tuesdays, Wednesdays, and Thursdays); plus shoe rental: $2

This place is pretty fun—and you'll even get some exercise. They've basically figured out how to put a bunch of trampolines together to make a couple of really big ones. There is a special toddler area for those under three (and you can still get on that and roll around with your kid). But the most fun are the big trampolines. Another great way to tire out your little girl or boy.

Fun Fact: Feeding your kid a lot of candy, ice cream, and Mexican food right before doing this is a really bad idea.

Bass Pro Shop

1365 South 5th Street   **St. Charles**
636-688-2500   **www.basspro.com**

Open: Monday–Saturday, 9 a.m. to 10 p.m.; Sunday, 10 a.m. to 7 p.m.; closed Christmas

Cost: Free! Unless you buy something for yourself, and how can you not?

Now lest your wife get suspicious of this outing, you show her this book, which validates this as a very dad-friendly thing to do with your kid. Educational as all get out, too. There's so much to look at! It's especially fun for kids in strollers (those just toddling will likely get into too much trouble). For total decadence, there's a Dairy Queen nearby—stop by there and get ice cream all over both your faces!

12 Playgrounds Worth the Drive

The St. Louis Greater Metro Area is blessed with terrific parks and playgrounds in every neighborhood, and no doubt you'll have staked out your favorites in the early stages of your dadness. However, let's not fall into a rut. On those days you get to spend more than just an hour with your Albert or Claire, here are some parks that are worth a longer drive for a new experience.

To get in the know about *all* the parks in the metro area, check out these websites:

St. Louis City: stlouis.missouri.org/citygov/parks

St. Louis County: www.co.st-louis.mo.us/parks

St. Charles County: parks.sccmo.org/parks

Jefferson County: www.jeffcomo.org/parks

Metro East: For park locations and amenities in Metro East towns, please visit the website for each respective city. Here are a few: www.aterloo.il.us/Recreation/Parks/Default.htm, www.collinsvillerec.com/Woodland.html, and www.belleville.net/departments/parks.asp

Des Peres Park
1050 Des Peres Road **Des Peres**
www.desperesmo.org

This park was rehabbed fairly recently and caters to all ages with multiple structures. There's also a play fountain. And while you may want to walk down to the lake's edge and look at the geese, you'd better not, unless you all want to get covered in goose droppings!

Lewis Park
Delmar at Yale **University City**

It's a little park, but with its fountains and frogs and fish it provides instant material for a small science lab. The playground is very accessible for little ones. And for fun afterward, head to the Loop for lunch or a snack at Fitz's!

Longview Farms Park
13525 Clayton Road   **Town & Country**
www.tandccityparks.org

A great playground is featured in this tucked-away gem of a park, along with a lake ringed by a kid-friendly, almost-mile-long trail.

Fun Fact: Native American remains are said to be buried here, but no bones or artifacts have ever been found. Still, there's nothing keeping you from picking up a rock and telling your kid it's a fossilized toenail.

Queeny Park
550 Weidman Road   **Chesterfield**
www.stlouisco.com/parks/queeny.html

A really unusual playground that is especially fun for the over three crowd is the big draw. There's fishing, trails, and even hayrides. Queeny is home to a lot of special events, including the Greater St. Louis Science Fair and various festivals. Call about the hayrides: 314.615.4386.

Fun Fact: It has a Dog Museum, which ironically, doesn't allow dogs.

St. Vincent Park
7335 St. Charles Rock Road   **North County**
www.stlouisco.com/parks/st-vincent.html

314.721.5702

St. Vincent has a great water park that is open to all residents of the metro St. Louis area and is very toddler/baby friendly.

Tilles Park
9551 Litzsinger Road   **Ladue**
www.co.st-louis.mo.us/parks/tilles.html

Children's Hospital teamed with Tilles to create a new all-inclusive playground in spring 2007, and it's now one of the best in the area. There are multiple play structures for all ages and physical abilities, a super-spongy rubberized floor, a sand area, and best of all, the Spray Plaza.

Tower Grove Park

4256 Magnolia Avenue   South St.
Louis City
www.towergrovepark.org

Nearly every weekend, Tower Grove Park plays host to a number of festivals and events, ranging from its weekly Saturday morning Farmer's Market (www.tgmarket.org) to international food festivals. Arm yourself with a gyro and set the young one loose on a playground or in the wading pool. Age-specific playgrounds flank the wading pool. Or grab a seat under a tree and watch a sporting event or team practice. You can educate your son in the finer points of kickball, corkball, and hurling in addition to the park sport standards.

Township Park

6364 Center Grove Road
Edwardsville, IL

This old-school wooden playground comes complete with tire climbs. You'll want to make sure your kid has shoes and socks on, and you probably want to make sure your kid is old enough to climb on things, as it can be frustrating to those just starting to toddle. Afterward, drive five minutes to the Dairy Queen downtown. Better yet, head to Annie's Frozen Custard stand which features kid's tables.

Turtle Park

Oakland and Tamm Avenues   Forest Park
stlouis.missouri.org/citygov/parks/forestpark/
turtle.html

A sentimental favorite, while not the greatest "playground" per se, it's a St. Louis institution that every dad should take his kid to at least once.

Veterans Memorial Park

2577 Redman Road   North County
www.stlouisco.com/parks/veterans   314.355.7374

A playground and fishing pond make this a great place to spend a nice morning or afternoon. There's also a children's play pool, which is free to tots under 4 (adults $4). The Eagle Springs Golf Course is right there, and really when you think about it, it's never too young to start training your kid to be a good caddy!

Vlasis Park

14811 Manchester Road   **Ballwin**
www.ballwin.mo.us/vlasis

Talk about a great, swim-diaper-friendly place. This playground not only has the always-appreciated rubberized ground, but all little kids love the splash fountains. The park also has a walking trail and a stocked pond, so consider packing a picnic and make a day of it! Guaranteed to tire out the most energetic kid.

Watson Trails Park

12450 W. Watson   **Sunset Hills**
www.sunset-hills.com/parks/system

Terrific smaller park for smaller kids and a playground that's appropriate for the young youngsters (too bad it doesn't have the rubberized ground covering though). Bring a small rod for your kid, as fishing permits are only a dollar. The hiking trails are good for the three and up crowd, and all lead back to the playground. Oh, and by all means, feed the ducks!

ACKNOWLEDGMENTS

To say this book would not be possible without my immensely brilliant and talented wife, Lauren, is an understatement—and not because she apparently had something to do in providing the two boys who inspired this book. Her support, editorial advice, and ability to say "that's not funny" was indispensable.

Thanks also to the good people at Reedy Press, particularly Matt Heidenry and Josh Stevens, who were critical in supplying the guidance, advice, nurturing, and prodding this humble tome required. Not just great publishers, they are both terrific dads and helped out above and beyond merely shepherding the book to publication.

I thank my playgroup for allowing me to be a part of the assemblage and getting to watch their terrific kids grow up in the last five years; I thank Cecily, Paco, Sam, Lily, Carter, Isabella, Finnegan, Lochlan, Fiona, and Ben. Without these kids, the book (and the perfection of the "Playdate/Happy Hour" combo) would not have been possible.

Other terrific friends and great parents who helped in ways they probably weren't aware of, or in some cases gave direct advice and ideas, include Gary Mays, Briana Hepfinger, John McMurray, Steve Kauffmann, and Barb Jochens. Extra thanks goes to my sister, Laurie Clark, the best aunt in the world.

Have to also send out a shout out to the good people working at the Webster Groves Starbucks, who kept me properly caffeinated as I sat with my laptop there working on this book for months.

And of course, I'm most grateful for my boys, Owen and Beckett.

Kevin M. Mitchell

About the Author

Kevin M. Mitchell grew up in South County (Lindbergh, Class of '81) and lived in Kansas City, San Francisco, and Los Angeles before returning to St. Louis in 2001. He writes books, plays, and magazine articles, and fronts a swingin' jazz quartet, the Kevin Mitchell 4. More important, he is a Stay At Home Dad (SAHD) to his two boys, Owen and Beckett. He loves writing about himself in the third person almost as much as he loves his wife, Lauren. He lives in Webster Groves.